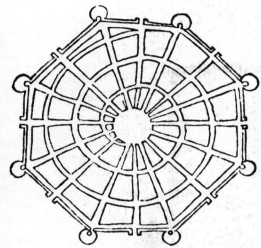

COLIN ROWE & FRED KOETTER

COLLAGE

The MIT Press, *Cambridge, Massachusetts, and London, England*

CITY

Contents

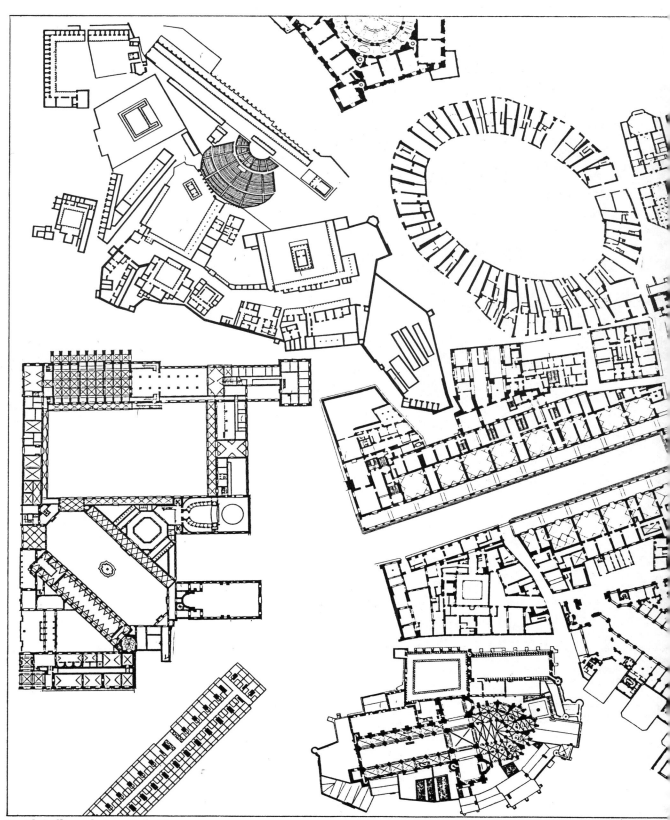

David Griffin and Hans Kolhoff:
City of composite presence

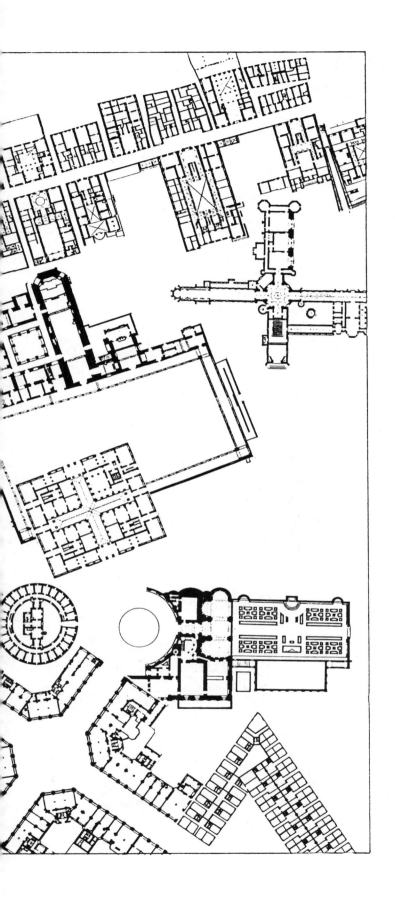

Collage City

Introduction

Man has a prejudice against himself; anything which is a product of his mind seems to him to be unreal or comparatively insignificant. We are satisfied only when we fancy ourselves surrounded by objects and laws independent of our nature. GEORGE SANTAYANA

But what is nature? Why is custom not natural? I greatly fear that this nature is itself only a first custom as custom is a second nature. BLAISE PASCAL

With these two statements—one a commentary upon inhibition and the other a question as to the eternal source of all authority—it might be possible to construct a theory of society and even a theory of architecture; but, if modesty restrains the attempt, there are also pragmatic reasons which make the same insistence.

The city of modern architecture (it may also be called the modern city) has not yet been built. In spite of all the good will and good intentions of its protagonists, it has remained either a project or an abortion; and, more and more, there no longer appears to be any convincing reason to suppose that matters will ever be otherwise. For the constellation of attitudes and emotions which are gathered together under the general notion of

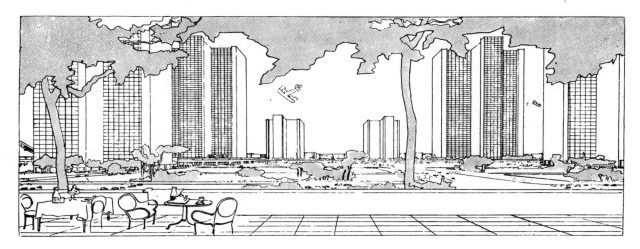

Le Corbusier: Ville Contemporaine, 1922

modern architecture and which then overflow, in one form or another, into the inseparably related field of planning, begin—in the end—to seem altogether too contradictory, too confused and too feebly unsophisticated to allow for any but the most minor productive results.

By one interpretation, modern architecture is a hard-headed and hard-nosed undertaking. There is a problem, a specific problem, and there is an obligation, an obligation to science, to solve it in all its particularity; and so, while without bias and embarrassment we proceed to scrutinize the facts, then, as we accept them, we simultaneously allow these hard empirical facts to dictate the solution. But, if such is one important and academically enshrined thesis, then, alongside it, there is to be recognized a no less respectable one; the proposition that modern architecture is the instrument of philanthropy, liberalism, the 'larger hope' and the 'greater good'.

In other words, and right at the beginning, one is confronted with the simultaneous profession of two standards of value whose compatibility is not evident. On the one hand, there is an expression of allegiance to the criteria of what—though disguised as science—is, after all, simply management; on the other, a devotion to the ideals of what was a few years ago often spoken of as the counter culture—life, people, community and all the rest; and that this curious dualism causes so little surprise can only be attributed to a determination not to observe the obvious.

But, if presumably the ultimate conflict which presents itself is that between a retarded conception of science and a reluctant recognition of poetics, this being said, it is apparent that modern architecture, in its great phase, was the great idea that it undoubtedly was precisely because it compounded and paraded to extravagance the two myths which it still

Le Corbusier: Plan Voisin, 1925

most publicly advertises. For if the combination of fantasies about science –with its objectivity–and fantasies about freedom–with its humanity– comprised one of the most appealing and pathetic of late nineteenth century doctrines, then the decisive twentieth century embodiment of these themes in the form of building could not fail to stimulate; and, the more it excited the imagination, the more the conception of a scientific, progressive and historically relevant architecture could only serve as a focus for a still further concentration of fantasy. The new architecture was rationally determinable; the new architecture was historically predestined; the new architecture represented the overcoming of history; the new architecture was responsive to the spirit of the age; the new architecture was socially therapeutic; the new architecture was young and, being self-renewing, it was never to be wearied by age; but–perhaps above all–the new architecture meant the end to deception, dissimulation, vanity, subterfuge and imposition.

Such were some of the subliminal suggestions which stimulated modern architecture and were, in turn, stimulated by it; and, as we look back on a doctrine so extraordinary and a message so bizarre, since we are speaking of a period now fifty years ago, we might also allow to come to mind Woodrow Wilson's hopes for democracy and diplomacy. We might briefly contemplate the American president's 'open contracts openly arrived at'. For from Woodrow Wilson's hopes for international politics to the *ville radieuse* is but the merest of steps. The crystal city and the dream of absolutely unconcealed negotiation (no playing of poker) both, alike, represented the total expulsion of evil after the purgation of war.

The ex-president of Princeton's dream, the pathetic by-product of a liberal Presbyterian faith which was both too good for this world and not good enough, which was only to be honoured in the breach, created its own portentous vacuum and devastation. By the exponents of *Realpolitik* he and what he represented were simply ignored or, at most, received a ritual deference which was worse than nothing; and, though the vision of the crystal city has enjoyed greater longevity, today its fate hardly seems to have been significantly more prosperous. For this was a city in which all authority was to be dissolved, all convention superseded; in which change was to be continuous and order, simultaneously, complete; in which the public realm, become superfluous, was to disappear and where the private realm, without further reason to excuse itself, was to emerge undisguised by the protection of façade. And now, even though the weight of the idea persists, it is a city which has shrunk to very little–to the impoverished banalities of public housing which stand around like the undernourished symbols of a new world which refused to be born.

Such has been the disintegration of an important frame of reference; and, like the idea of World War I as a war to end war, the city of modern architecture, both as psychological construct and as physical model, has been rendered tragically ridiculous. But, if so much is generally felt and if the urban model which achieved its decisive formulation give or take a

New York, public housing in Lower Manhattan

few years *c.* 1930 is now everywhere under attack, it is not very clear that either unorganized sentiment or self-conscious criticism has, so far, achieved any significant or comprehensive replacement. In fact, rather the reverse seems to have taken place. For, while the city of Ludwig Hilberseimer and Le Corbusier, the city celebrated by CIAM and advertised by the Athens Charter, the former city of deliverance, is every day found increasingly inadequate, apparently its very expediency guarantees its adulterated and all-devouring growth. So much so, that it might be believed that what here presents itself is a spectacle of spontaneous generation, a never-to-be-imagined nightmare and a wholly mindless version of Daniel Burnham's 'a noble diagram which once registered will never die'.

And accordingly, the present situation is knotted and almost insoluble. For the two increasingly desperate 'obligations' of the architect—on the one hand to 'science' and on the other to 'people'—continue to persist; and, as their old working symbiosis of the twenties becomes ever more shaky, these divergent drives acquire a literalness and a vehemence which begin to cancel out the usefulness of either. So modern architecture, professing to be scientific, displayed a wholly naïve idealism. So let this situation be corrected; and, from now on let us increasingly consult technology, behaviourist research and the computer. Or, alternatively, modern architecture, professing to be humane, displayed a wholly unacceptable and sterile scientific rigour. Therefore, from now on, let us desist from intellectualist vanity and let us be content to replicate things as they are, to observe a world unreconstructed by the arrogance of would-be philosophers but as the mass of humanity prefers it to be—useful, real and densely familiar.

Now, which of these two prospective programmes for the future—the despotism of 'science' or the tyranny of the 'majority'—is the more completely repulsive is difficult to say; but that, taken separately or together, they can only extinguish all initiative should not require inordinate emphasis. Nor should it be necessary to say that these alternatives—*Let science build the town* and *Let people build the town*—are both of them profoundly neurotic. For, up to a point, science will and should build the town and, up to a point, so will and should collective opinion; but the never ending insistence on the incompetence of the architect, which increasingly becomes more true and which is a continuous insistence on the evil of self-conscious activity, should at least be recognized for the psychological manoeuvre that it is—as a guilt-ridden attempt to shift the locus of responsibility.

But, if the architect's social guilt and the means he has employed to effect its sublimation is a whole story which has resulted in the complete disarray of the profession, more important is that we are here once more in the presence of Santayana's 'the human mind has a prejudice against itself' and, alongside this deep-seated prejudice, we confront the corresponding determination to pretend that human artifacts can be

top left
Paris, La Défense

top right
Paris, Bobigny

below
St Louis, demolition of Pruit-Igoe housing, 1971

other than what they are. And, of course, given the anxiety to induce such illusion, the appropriate mechanism will never be lacking. For there is, after all, always 'nature'; and some concept of nature will always be invented—discovered is the operative word—in order to appease the pangs of conscience.

With so much said an initiatory argument is almost complete. For, on the whole, the twentieth century architect has been entirely unwilling to consider the ironies of Pascal's question; and the idea that nature and custom may be interconnected is, of course, entirely subversive of his position. Nature is pure, custom corrupt; and the obligation to transcend custom is not to be evaded.

Now, in its day, this was an important concept; and, as a conviction that only the new is fully authentic, one may still feel its cogency. However, whatever may be the authenticity of the new, alongside novelty of artifacts one might just possibly recognize novelty of ideas; and the twentieth century architect's working ideas have, for a very long time remained conspicuously without overhaul. There persists an eighteenth century belief in the veracity of science (Bacon, Newton?) and an equally eighteenth century belief in the veracity of the collective will (Rousseau, Burke?); and, if both of these can be conceived to be furnished with persuasive Hegelian, Darwinian, Marxian overtones, then there the situation rests, almost as it rested nearly one hundred years ago. Which is, very largely, a notion of the architect as a sort of human ouija-board or planchette, as a sensitive antenna who receives and transmutes the logical messages of destiny.

'It is the mark of an educated man to look for precision in each class of things just as far as the nature of the subject admits.'[1] It is hard to disagree; but, in the endeavour to provide architecture and urbanism with a precision that, of their nature, they can scarcely possess, the guidance of eighteenth century 'nature' has been all too well consulted; and, meanwhile (with the architect absorbed with visions of super-'science' or 'unconscious' self-regulation, with a make-believe unprecedented for absence of effectiveness) in a kind of resurgence of Social Darwinism—natural selection and the survival of the fittest—the rape of the great cities of the world proceeds.

There remains the old and enticing advice that, if rape is inevitable, then get with it and enjoy; but, if this central creed of Futurism—let us celebrate *force majeure*—is unacceptable to the moral consciousness, then we are obliged to think again. Which is what the present essay is all about.' A proposal for constructive dis-illusion, it is simultaneously an appeal for order and disorder, for the simple and the complex, for the joint existence of permanent reference and random happening, of the private and the public, of innovation and tradition, of both the retrospective and the prophetic gesture. To us the occasional virtues of the modern city seem to be patent and the problem remains how, while allowing for the need of a 'modern' declamation, to render these virtues responsive to circumstance.

Utopia: Decline and Fall?

For unto you is paradise opened, the tree of life is planted, the time to come is prepared, plenteousness is made ready, a city is builded, and rest is allowed, yea perfect goodness and wisdom.

The root of evil is sealed up from you, weakness and the moth is hid from you, and corruption is fled into hell to be forgotten.

Sorrows are passed, and in the end is shewed the treasure of immortality.
2 ESDRAS 8: 52-4

Where we do not reflect on myth but truly live in it there is no cleft between the actual reality of perception and the world of mythical fantasy. ERNST CASSIRER

Bruno Taut: design from Alpine Architektur, 1919

Modern architecture is surely most cogently to be interpreted as a gospel—as, quite literally, a message of good news; and hence its impact. For, when all the smoke clears away, its impact may be seen as having very little to do with either its technological innovations or its formal vocabulary. Indeed the value of these could never have been so much what they seemed to be as what they signified. Their appearance was a thinly disguised alibi; and, essentially, they were didactic illustrations, to be apprehended not so much for themselves but as the indices of a better world, of a world where rational motivation would prevail and where all the more visible institutions of the political order would have been swept into the irrelevant limbo of the superseded and the forgotten. And hence modern architecture's former heroic and exalted tone. Its aim was never to provide a well-cushioned accommodation for either private or public bourgeois euphoria. Instead, its ideal, which was thought to be far more important, was to exhibit the virtues of an apostolic poverty, of a quasi-Franciscan *Existenz minimum*. 'For it is easier for a camel to go through a needle's eye, than for a rich man to enter into the kingdom of God;' and, with this belligerent and somewhat *samurai* dictum in mind, the austerity of the twentieth century architect must be abundantly explained. He was helping to establish and to celebrate an enlightened and a just society; and one definition of modern architecture might be that it was an attitude towards building which was divulging in the present that more perfect order which the future was about to disclose.

> He (the architect) will build his rampart out of the Will. He will conquer the centripetal spirits of the air, stretch and spring over the ether mantle which envelops him like a skin, shed layer after layer and climb higher and purer over and above each of these transcended remains... Thousands of naked souls, thousands of lesser souls and diminished souls await the goal which should gape in front of them, the kingdom of heaven on earth.[1]

With these words of Hermann Finsterlin, placed centre scene in the ethos of German Expressionism, one is empowered to sense its ecstatic motivations and chiliastic drive; but, though one may wish to restrict an interpretation of what is here read, it is also to be doubted whether this is possible. For, while extreme in all its naked extravagance, this statement also provides an hysterical condensation of much of what was said with more circumspection elsewhere. Alter the form of words only a little and one is admitted to the mood of Hannes Meyer and Walter Gropius. Alter it only a little more and the moods of Le Corbusier and Lewis Mumford will begin to emerge. Scratch the surface of modern architecture's matter of factness, simply for a moment doubt its ideals of objectivity, and almost invariably, subsumed beneath the veneers of rationalism, there is to be found that highly volcanic species of psychological lava which, in the end, is the substratum of the modern city.

Now the ecstatic component of modern architecture has received a completely insufficient attention. Nor should it be very necessary to say

Sir Thomas More: frontispiece from *Utopia*, 1516

why. An apparently rational justification has been taken, for the most part, at its face value; but, if the architect and his apologist have been pre-eminently concerned with 'facts', it should still be evident that no scientific explanation of the modern movement will ever be possible so long as the architect's overt and entire reasonableness continues to remain an issue which is felt to require establishment. Frank Lloyd Wright's 'In this way I saw the architect as the saviour of the culture of modern American society, saviour now as for all civilisations heretofore'[2] and Le Corbusier's 'On the day when contemporary society, at present so sick, has become properly aware that only architecture and city planning can provide the exact prescription for its ills, then the day will have come for the great machine to be put in motion'[3] for all of what now seems to be their utter grotesqueness, these are statements of far more explanatory power than the whole still-prevalent apparatus of exegesis. More explanatory because they disclose something of the architect's state of mind and make evident a quality of messianic passion, an anxiety both to end the world and begin it anew, which must surely have acted as some sort of intellectual distorting lens, enlarging or diminishing whatever material—whether formal or technological—it made visible and was, therefore, able to make useful.

We are speaking of a psychological condition of the greatest significance, of one of those elemental and eruptive occasions when the impossible re-directs the real, or when the expectation of the millennial kingdom subverts all reasonable probability; and if, in writing about late mediaeval chiliasm, Karl Mannheim has insisted on exactly these qualities, on a radical fusion of 'spiritual fermentation and physical excitement',[4] we wish only to call attention to the one-time elevation of the architect's fantasy, to notice some of its causes and, later, to comment upon the subsequent devolution.

For which purpose, and particularly since we are speaking of cities, there are two stories: the first that of 'the classical utopia, the criticial utopia inspired by universal rational morality and ideas of justice, the Spartan and ascetic utopia which was already dead before the French Revolution'[5]; and the second that of the activist utopia of the post-Enlightenment.

The story of the classical utopia of *c.* 1500 scarcely requires inordinate explanation. A city of the mind, ultimately compounded of Hebraic apocalyptic and platonic cosmology, its ingredients are never far to seek; and, whatever other pre-disposing causes one might choose to find, fundamentally, one will still be left with either Plato heated up via the Christian message or the Christian message cooled down via Plato. Whatever qualifications may be added, it will still be *Revelation* plus *The Republic* or the *Timaeus* plus a vision of the New Jerusalem.

Now, even five hundred years ago, this was scarcely a highly original conflation; and therefore it should not be surprising that the classical utopia never displayed that explosive component, that sense of an

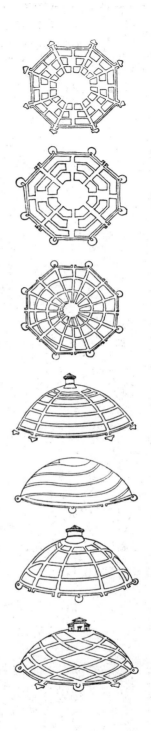

Francesco di Giorgio Martini: studies for ideal cities

impending and all transforming new order which belongs to the utopian myth as it was received by the early twentieth century. And, instead, if one chooses to inspect it, the classical utopia will offer itself largely as an object of contemplation. Its mode of existence will be quiet and, maybe, even a little ironical. It will behave as a detached reference, as an informing power, as rather more of an heuristic device than any form of directly applicable political instrument.

An icon of the good society, the terrestrial shadow of an idea, the classical utopia was, necessarily, addressed to a conspicuously small audience; and its architectural corollary, the ideal city– no less an emblem of universal and final good–is to be imagined as an instrument of education addressed to an equally limited clientèle. As with the advice of Machiavelli, the ideal city of the Renaissance was primarily a vehicle for the provision of information to the prince; and, as extension of this, it was also an agent for the maintenance and decorous representation of the state. Social criticism it no doubt was; but it still offered not so much a future ideal as an hypothetical one. The icon was to be adored and was–up to a point–to be used; but as image rather than prescription. And, like Castiglione's image of the courtier, the ideal city always allowed itself simply to be observed and enjoyed for its own sake.

As a reference and no more than this, both utopia and the ideal city, the combination–however belated–of Filarete and Castiglione, of More and Machiavelli, of manners and morals, produced results. It was a combination which sponsored a convention; and then a convention which, while it did not seriously alleviate the social order, became responsible for the form of cities which are still today admired. To be very brief: it was a combination which acted to substitute the formula of Serlio's Tragic Scene for that of his Comic, a convention which insinuated itself into

Sebastiano Serlio:

left
Comic Scene

right
Tragic Scene

existing situations in order to convert a world of random and mediaeval happening into a more highly integrated situation of dignified and serious deportment.

Now, whether this preference for the classical rules and by-products of tragic drama was good or bad is not an issue. But, evidently, it represented only a temporary situation; and, in the end, the metaphysical aloofness of the classical utopia was not to be sustained. Private glimpses of final goodness could only encourage a public appetite; and, as the stock of the prince and what he represented began to fall, so his strange models of round towns and the ideas they implicated also became scheduled for massive revision. For now, as the populace increasingly entered the picture, not only the idea but also the empirical condition of society became of significance. Interest was re-directed; and, as abstract notions of morality were softened by the demand that morality should become real, so the contemplative platonic model yielded to a far more energetic utopian directive. It yielded to a message which could be interpreted not merely as a critical reference for the few but which could be seen as a vehicle for the literal deliverance and transformation of society as a whole.

Such a vision, the basis of the activist utopia of the post-Enlightenment, was presumably first solidly fuelled by the stimulus of Newtonian rationalism. For, if the properties and behaviour of the material world had at last become explicable without resort to dubious speculation, if they were now provable by observation and experiment, then, as the measurable could increasingly be equated with the real, so it became possible to conceive the ideal city of the mind as presently to be cleansed of all metaphysical and superstitious cloudiness. Such was the scale of the venture. It was no small undertaking. But, if a Newton could conclusively demonstrate the rational construction of the physical world, then why should the inner workings of the mind and, better still, the workings of society not become equally demonstrable. Via a fully orchestrated appeal to reason and to experimental philosophy, via rejection of received and apparently arbitrary authority, it was surely possible that society and the human condition could be remade and become subject to laws quite as infallible as those of physics. Then—and soon—it would no longer be necessary for the ideal city to be simply a city of the mind.

But, if an overwhelming belief in the possibility of a rational society was short lived, if isolated doubts were very early entertained, a compelling interest in the creation of a harmonious and wholly just social order more than held its own; and, as it moved—still somewhat mechanically—towards the nineteenth century, this now much more literal utopian fantasy was enabled to acquire a spiritual substance and dynamic. For, if the workings of society were ever to be placed upon a basis of firm establishment, it was surely necessary that, just as the exponents of what amounted to scientific revolution had scrutinized simply nature, so the exponents of social renovation should scrutinize 'natural' society. And 'natural' society as the paradigm of 'rational' society could only lead to the examination of 'natural' man.

Indeed, in order that society be subjected to successful analysis, it was essential that a primary model of man be adequately isolated and identified. Man must be stripped of his cultural contaminations and social corruptions. He must be imagined in his aboriginal condition, placed at point zero, before Temptation, before the Fall. And it is against such a backdrop, an inextinguishable drive for reason and innocence, that the eighteenth century delivered its most earth-shaking fabrication—the myth of the noble savage.

In one form or another the myth of the noble savage had, of course, already enjoyed an extended history. For the innocent natural man is first of all the decorative inhabitant of the idealized pastoral arcadia; and if as such he had been very well-known to Antiquity, after his Renaissance re-entry upon the stage of culture he could only become an increasingly useful moral accessory. But, though an intrusion into the mechanical system of things, the natural man (an abstraction which was felt to be real) was almost too completely made to order for the Enlightenment. Made to order not only because he could be presented as that universally valid specimen of mankind which science so badly required; but, more importantly, because a slightly tuned up and modified version of the noble savage could very well serve as a much needed component in the putting together of a reasonably elevated conception of common man. There was common man, a worth-while object of responsible consideration,

The Natural Man: from F. O. C. Darley,
Scenes from Indian Life, 1844

The Natural Man: from Le Corbusier,
Oeuvre Complète, 1910–1929

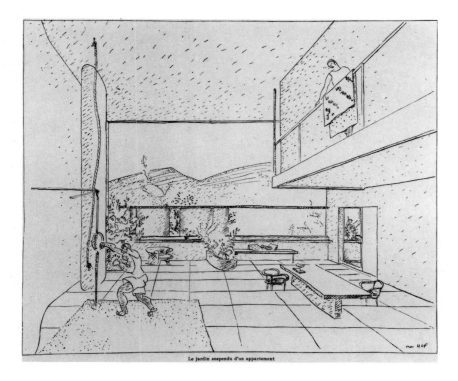

Le jardin suspendu d'un appartement

but a neglected, flat, anonymous and distinctly unheroic character. There was his deplorable and genuine plight; there was the question of his promotion which badly required both pedigree and colour; and, hence, there was a function for the noble savage who was able to provide more than sufficient amounts of both.

Once admitted to civilized society as something other than a literary convention, it was inevitable that the noble savage should be destined to a brilliant career. An abstraction he might be; but he was also nothing if not protean and dynamic. And certainly he turns out to have been a superlative role player—a classical shepherd, a Red Indian, someone discovered by Captain Cook, a *sans culotte* of 1792, a participant in the July Revolution, a denizen of Merrie England (or any other Gothic society), a Marxian proletarian, a Mycenaean Greek, a modern American, any old peasant, a liberated hippy, a scientist, an engineer and, in the end, a computer. As critic of culture and society, a useful presumption for conservatives and radicals alike, in the last two hundred years the noble savage has surrendered himself to the widest variety of performances; and in each performance, while it lasted, his activity has never been less than convincing.

But, considering the noble savage as a purveyor of innocence, it is obvious that, in bringing together the utopian and the arcadian myths, the Enlightenment was responsible for a decisive and fertile act of misce-

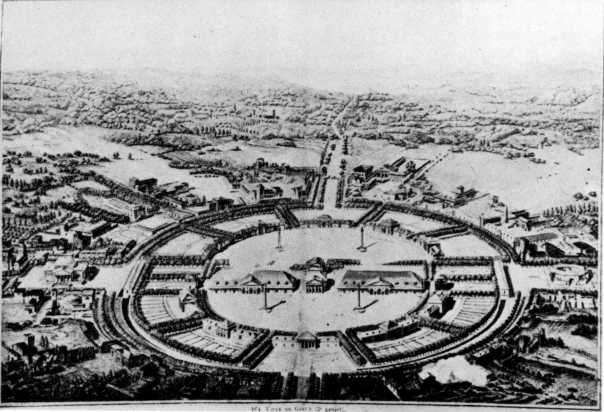

LA VILLE DE CHAUX (2ᵉ projet).

genation. For the two myths simultaneously corroborate and contradict each other. The one relates to an end of history and the other to a beginning; utopia celebrates the triumphs of constraint—even of repression—while arcadia involves the pre-civilized blessings of freedom; in Freudian language the one is all super-ego the other all id; but, nevertheless, the two myths experienced each other's fatal attraction; and if, after their linkage, nothing could ever be quite the same again, it is towards this typically eighteenth century liaison that we might look for at least some explanation of what was now to be the ongoing change in utopia's morale.

As a protagonist of a myth related to the beginning of time, the more the noble savage could be felt to be a real and an historic figure, then the more it became possible to imagine him as reproducible; and the more it thereby became reasonable to envisage the good society as a prospective rather than an hypothetical condition, the more utopia was encouraged to abandon platonic reserve for political passion.

However, while Enlightenment criticism clearly modified the content of utopia it exercised conspicuously little influence upon the form; and, whatever the activities of the noble savage may have been, utopia's continuing preoccupation with classical figure and decorum is one of the more notable characteristics of its early activist phase. The agreed and recognized utopian convention persisted; and thus, for instance, the ideal city of André *c.* 1870 (an influence of Fourierist speculation?)[6] is no more dramatically deviant from *quattrocento* prototype than is Ledoux's project of 1776 for his industrial settlement at Chaux. Nevertheless—and even at Chaux—there is a breach which has been made. For, whatever its unlikely format, La Saline de Chaux is a proposal dedicated to the service of production; and, if its circular configuration may be construed as a tribute to the mythic potency of the classical utopia, it is still a distinctly subversive tribute. Simply the manager has pre-empted the place of the prince; and, if it is now not the law-giver but *le directeur* who is the informing power of the city, it is just possible that we are here, very incipiently, presented with a new idea for the constitution of the state.

But, obviously, this is not the only way in which Chaux is to be read as a criticism of the traditional image; and, if we can have no doubt that the noble savage (supplied by Rousseau) lurks in the naturalistic environs, we can also be fairly certain that the circular dispensation is intended to evoke not so much the ancient authority of Plato as the present eminence of Newton. For this was a time when monuments to Newton were about to abound; and to move from Ledoux's Chaux to Saint Simon's proposal of 1803 for a Grand Council of Newton is merely to follow a tendency.

Henri de Saint-Simon (1760-1825) may be thought to have aspired to become a Newton of the political realm and his proposal was for a universal ruling body. Existing authority was condemned by its idiosyncrasies and, in its place, there was to be established a world govern-

left above
André: a mid-19th century project for an ideal community

left below
Claude-Nicolas Ledoux: project for La Saline de Chaux, 1776

Etienne-Louis Boullée: project for Cenotaph to Newton, c.1784

ment of scientists, mathematicians, scholars, artists, who were to propagate the cause of Newton—and reason—and everywhere erect temples to the cult. The proposal, published in *Lettres d'un habitant de Genève à ses contemporains*,[7] was madly academic if not a little demented; but, whatever may have been its extravagance, in its irrational exaltation of reason it prepared the way for momentous happenings. For, with the Saint-Simonian motto that 'the golden age is not behind us but in front of us and that (it) will be realized by the perfection of the social order',[8] it is evident that the whole moral stance of the classical utopia has become effectively superseded. In other words, we are here at the point of turnover; and the activist utopia, utopia as 'a blueprint for the future' has finally made its decisive appearance. In a world of what was unprecedented scientific growth, the logical organization of society is felt to be imminent and therefore an ideal of *positive* social purpose must now be stipulated which, inspired by the triumphs of science, must be directed towards placing the 'science of man' on a basis absolutely beyond conjecture. The need is evident and hence the attempt must be made to establish science as the foundation of morals, to turn politics into a branch of physics and, ultimately, to enjoin the replacement of arbitrary government by the rule of rational administration.

Such were some of the Saint-Simonian ideas as they became developed over the next twenty or so years—a well-intentioned attempt to 'replace the government of man by the administration of things'. In spite of Saint-Simon's authoritarianism, his ideas are equipped with obviously gratifying social overtones—and, not least, for the arts. In the rational society production will prosper and, with this diffused prosperity, the arts will converge both to sponsor and to corroborate the new establishment. Such was the prospect. The alliance between progressive art and progressive society (all knowledge acting in concert) appears to have been one of the central intuitions of Saint-Simon's creed; and as being so was reflected by his disciples.

Art, the expression of society, manifests, in its highest soaring, the most advanced social tendencies: it is the forerunner and the revealer. Therefore to know whether art fulfils its proper mission as initiator, whether the artist is truly of the *avant garde*, one must know where Humanity is going, know what the destiny of the Human race is.[9]

And, if a statement of this kind is impossible to imagine without the influence of Saint-Simon, then we may also introduce another equally 'modern' proposition of some twenty years earlier. Driven by comparable convictions the poet Léon Halévy confesses his belief that the time is close when 'the artist will possess the power to please and to move (the masses) with the same certainty as the mathematician solves a geometrical problem or the chemist analyses some substance'; and then only, he continues, 'will the moral side of society be firmly established'.[10]

But, if such declarations seem to bring us immensely close to the utopian inflammation which characterized the early twentieth century, one is still obliged to contemplate the relative sterility of French Positivism as an influence isolated by itself. For, whatever might be said about Saint-Simon, about the subsequent developments of Auguste Comte, about the parallel contributions of Charles Fourier and the rest, it can only be to recognize that, by and in themselves, these persons represented something of an historical cul-de-sac. In full nineteenth century they were operating in a version of the Enlightenment tradition; and necessarily, for better or worse, this tradition had begun to wear thin.

On the one hand, in a world where expanding markets could only incite the banker and the industrialist to enthusiasm, the purely intellectual optimism of the eighteenth century began to seem gratuitous; and on the other, at least in England and Germany, it had long been apparent that society could scarcely be the mechanical construct which French rationalism, apart from Rousseau, had wished to suppose. Instead, in both England and Germany, Rousseau's noble savage had long been regarded not so much as an abstraction which might facilitate rationalist argument; but rather as some sort of atavistic race memory, the very existence of which was a commentary upon the inadequacy of French pattern making. For, in both countries, under Romantic and *Sturm und Drang* influences, it was not so much an idea of mankind in the abstract as of society or the state in all their historical specificity which had begun to prevail; and, in both cases, the bias of this argument was to presume the notion of society as organic growth rather than French mechanism. The ultimate contributions to the argument were, of course, German and were to culminate in the Hegelian conception of historical dialectic; but the spectacular polemics of its important English phase can scarcely be overlooked. And the reference here is to Edmund Burke and his *Reflections on the Revolution in France*.[11]

Now Burke's reputation has always been ambiguous. Aesthetic theorist—political philosopher: which is he? But, if Burke possesses further notoriety as a founder of modern conservatism, it also cannot be difficult to see how elements of his thought were able to embed themselves in the English socialist tradition. Such a utopia as William Morris's *News from Nowhere*,[12] wholly lacking in elements of classical format, might, for instance, be considered as finally derivative from Burkean influence; and, in any case, as with Morris at a later date, Burke's lack of interest in the potential of either science or industrial growth must be considered one of the negative distinctions of his position. He recoils from any ideas of simple utility—one imagines an older Burke and a younger Bentham as antitheses—and, like so many of his German contemporaries, reacting against the tradition of the Enlightenment, he makes his appeal to the imponderable and the not-to-be analysed, 'to what is so much out of fashion in Paris, I mean to experience.'[13]

Logically, one might feel that Burke should have been highly inspired by the French Revolution. For, if back in 1757, there he was—in full pursuit of the Sublime,[14] then, by 1792 there he was—certainly presented with an exhibition of the Sublime in action. But instead, of course, Burke reacted against his earlier intuitions. 'A strange, nameless, wild, enthusiastic thing', such was the Revolution. A case of abstract and tyrannical reason invading the prerogatives of established prescription, if this was an instance of Rousseau's 'general will', then Burke—who had his opinions in common with Rousseau—had very little use for it; and, for him, if society was indeed a contract, this was no imaginary legal document which happened to have gotten lost. Rather it was the accumulated traditions of a given society at a given time, traditions which should guarantee the specific exercise of liberty, but which should be understood to transcend any private and individual exercise of reason.

In such ways the appeal to experience became an appeal to the state as instrument of Providence and to history as concrete spectacle of social evolution. 'Without . . . civil society man could not by any possibilities arrive at the perfection of which his nature is capable';[15] but, if with these remarks the noble savage is encouraged to leave the drawing-room, his memory persists as that of an ancestor who can only be respected. For civil society is: 'a partnership in all science; . . . in all art; . . . in every virtue, and in all perfection . . . a partnership not only between those who are living, but between those who are living, those who are dead, and those who are to be born.'[16] In other words, civil society is a continuum which can barely be interrupted.

These were some of the very anti-utopian sentiments, partly coercive, partly libertarian, of which Burke delivered himself, and their effect was certainly double-edged. For in throwing his own version of history in the face of French rationalism Burke was contributing, it may be argued, quite as much to the developed activist utopia as did those doctrines which he was at so much effort to condemn. For we should now consider the organicist conception of society as becoming diffused throughout Romantic criticism; we should imagine the Saint-Simonian disciples gradually deserting the less pragmatic aspects of their leader's cause; we should notice their propensity to become Second Empire industrialists; and we should then recognize how, by the mid-nineteenth century, the Positivist utopia must have come to seem elaborately constricted. The Positivists might well have been concerned with erecting a political order upon 'scientific demonstrations totally independent of human will';[17] but, in spite of this programme, as the nineteenth century became increasingly drenched with notions of historical development, any simple ideas as to the 'wilful' and the 'scientific' were to become increasingly compromised.

In fact, by the mid-century, what Marx chose to designate Utopian Socialism may be felt to have disclosed itself in its characteristic architectural propositions. Fourier's Phalanstery of 1829, in which a simulacrum of Versailles is to be a prototype for the proletarian future, is only too symptomatic of the condition; and it should not be necessary to intrude Anglo-American and Owenite instances of roughly comparable proposals to make the point. 'Pocket editions of the New Jerusalem' as

Marx found them to be, for all their virtues, these are prosaic and un-evocative statements; and in an age of evolutionary aspiration and democratic upsurge, they were lacking in the comprehensiveness to convince.

At this stage an illustration might be allowed to infiltrate a commentary. Delacroix's superb allegory of July 1830, his *Liberty Leading the*

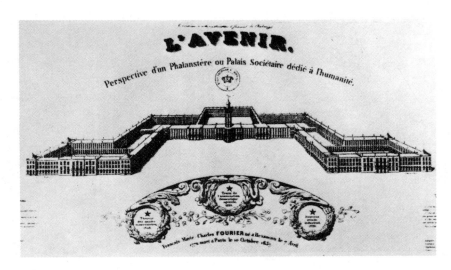

above
Charles Fourier: Phalanstery, 1829

below
Versailles, air view

Delacroix: Liberty leading the people,
1830

People, not only in its rhetoric but also in its size, may be considered
indicative of that newly liberated sweep of emotions and ideas which
Burke had recognized with alarm but which the Positivists had failed to
accommodate. For this is politics gone beyond politics. It is the crowd
inflamed by the dynamic of movement and destiny; the noble savage
dispossessed of his proper heritage and consumed by that vision of
emancipation which the eighteenth century had rendered substantial.
But, whatever else it may be, this heroic tumult of the barricades is totally
remote from the ethos of Positivism which—since we are dealing with
illustrations—is more obviously to be represented by a picture of forty years
earlier.

David's study for his never painted *Oath of the Tennis Court* is an
altogether different conception of heroics. The occasion is the opening act

of the revolution, 20 June 1789, when the Third Estate resolved never to disband until it had obtained its purpose. The setting, the *jeu de paume* at Versailles, is appropriately Spartan; and the personalities are significantly privileged. There can be no doubt about their habitual and everyday decorum; and, if the wind of change causes the curtains to billow in sympathetic response to group excitement, then, whatever the imminent drama may be, one is disposed to believe it can only involve the educated. Thomas Jefferson, one imagines, could have been present here; and, indeed, it is not very hard to suppose the whole scene as shifted to Philadelphia during the time of the Continental Congress. Concerned with the declaration of eternal truths, of self-evident doctrine, of principles valid in all times and in all places, this assembly of excited lawyers is about to indulge in everything which Burke chose to criticize; and, if there is that ominous movement of the curtains, then it is to be doubted whether these individuals would ever ascribe the cause to any impending historical storm.

The comparison, although it may speak for itself, is perhaps a little banal; but, if it might help to locate the Positivists in a cautious Restoration-Biedermayer milieu, then Delacroix's image of Liberty and the People might still be brought into confrontation with yet another image. And, in this case, there can be no people involved.

Upsurge, movement, the celebration of the irresistible, simple dynamic, a recognition of the predestined, all of these qualities are to be found represented in the city of Sant'Elia. Delacroix's dramatis personae of excited proletarians and infatuated students has become an assemblage of equally excited buildings, and, if we contemplate this genuinely first of

David: The Oath of the Tennis Court, 1791

The city of Sant' Elia-Mario Chiattone:
an aspect of the new city, 1914

activist utopian icons and observe to what degree Delacroix's rhetoric has
been transformed, to what degree the liberal 'power to the people' has
become power to the dynamo and power to the piston, then, while we
may recognize Sant'Elia's general descent from Saint-Simon we may still

be concerned with how this transformation was effected.

Delacroix, David, Sant'Elia, brought into such close proximity and obliged to behave as disputants in a history of ideas should be indicative of the cinematic method which is here pursued; but they may also be allowed to indicate its bias and direction, because, as here constructed, the route from Delacroix to Sant'Elia, if it does not lie via Marx, lies almost certainly via a conflation of ideas comparable to those which Marx deployed. In other words—and whether Sant'Elia was aware of it or not—the route probably lies via some interaction of the relative statics of Saint-Simon and Comte with the explicit dynamics of the Hegelian world view.

But the approach to Hegel, whose ideas are surely an indispensable component of the early twentieth century utopia, is attended with the most massive difficulty—with pain.[18] Historical inevitability, historical dialectic, the progressive revelation of the Absolute in history, the spirit of the age or the race or the people: we are dimly aware of how much these are the outcroppings of a theory of society as growth and, also, of how much less visible is their influence than that of theories of purely classical or French provenance. For, like Burke, Hegel was also concerned with the analysis of material which scarcely yields itself to existing rationalist technique or terminates in any tangible image.

However, central to his position, there would seem to be the concept that reason itself possesses no accessible stability. But, if this is the idea of an aggressively mobile and energetic reason, it is also equipped with the proviso that such reason is not so much a human product as it is the activity of a spiritual essence. 'Reason is the Sovereign of the World'; and, apparently, an absolute sovereign who inflexibly insists on the relatedness of all phenomena. But 'the term world includes both physical and psychical nature: There is the 'natural material universe' and the 'historical spiritual universe'; and since 'the world is not abandoned to chance and external contingent causes . . . [but] a Providence controls it', it follows that this Providence manifests itself not only in external nature but, even more significantly in Universal History. In other words, a divine and therefore rational creation is still in process; and, if 'the spiritual is the substantial world and the physical remains subordinate to it'—and if, simultaneously, history *must* be rational—then human passions, volitions, constructs are to be valued as the 'instruments and means of the World-Spirit for attaining its object'.

So much the fundamental doctrine would seem to be; and it is in such ways that nature, seen as history, is made to yield the spectacle of a divinely inspired and necessary drama. It is a fundamentally self-propelling drama proceeding towards a happy ending; but it is also a performance proceeding via the ceaseless interaction of affirmation and contradiction and, since we are immersed in its action, then the best we can do is to understand it. In fact freedom, which is an aspect of spirit, imposes the enterprise; and, if it is only through the activity of the historical consciousness that we, as captives of this freedom, can know

the substance of things, then it must also be in terms of this consciousness that liberty defines itself. Though, whatever this liberty may be, it
is still faced with yielding–even when achieved–to the endless prospect
of emerging and self-developing constellations of particulars, all of them
equipped with 'reason' and 'spirit' and all of them insisting on accommodation.

But, if the mere contemplation of Hegel may oblige agreement with
one of his first English admirers that his was 'a scrutiny of thought
so profound that it was for the most part unintelligible', it is not so
much his opacity that concerns us as his influence. 'Architecture is the
will of an epoch translated into space; living, changing, new;' 'the new
architecture is the inevitable logical product...of our age;' the architect's task consists in coming into agreement with the orientation of his
epoch....;'[19] these statements, respectively of Mies Van der Rohe,
Gropius and Le Corbusier, are perfectly illustrative of the manner in
which Hegelian categories and modes came gradually to saturate all
thought; and, if they seem never to have been interpreted in this context,
they are only cited here to indicate the relevance of Hegel as a continuing presence in the early twentieth century utopia. For, in all three
cases, an irresistible, coercive and logical 'history' seems to have become
quite as real as anything equipped with dimension, weight, colour,
texture.

However, this is to parenthesize. One is immediately faced with a
body of ideas relating to measurement and mechanism and another
body of ideas relating to change and organism. On the one hand, there
are to be found notions of society as potentially logical–in terms of
physics–and, on the other, as inherently logical–in terms of history.
There are statements as to the possibility of a scientific politics–independent of human will; and there are further statements as to the certainty
of a rational history–also independent of human intervention. There is
an older intellectualist mode and a newer historicist mode and which
of these attitudes is the more conservative or the more radical has now
become very difficult to say. Such as it is, Hegel's progressivism is sombre
and a little unctuous–very far indeed from Saint-Simon's complex of
science and secularism; but, if one were to subscribe to Hegel's own
conception of historical dialectic, one might presumably recognize that
what there could be here is a presentation of thesis and antithesis about
to interact.

Which, to be very brief, is surely how both systems were envisaged
by Marx; and the Marxian discrimination of 'structure' and 'superstructure' could only make a crucial contribution to his prospective
synthesis. For, if after 1848, the disillusioned mid-nineteenth century
rapidly turned from 'ideas' and optimism to 'facts' and force, from the
superfluous to the basic (one thinks of Bazarov in Turgenev's *Fathers
and Sons*), then if one stripped away the trivialities of French rationalism
and the pseudo-profundities of German involvement with *Geist*, if one

examined the real rather than the illusory, one would arrive at a true cognition of society's ultimate material base. One would perceive the essential naked 'structure', undistorted by the manipulators of the 'superstructure'. That is, by the representatives of religion and law, politics and art.

Or at least, something like this combination of French scientism and German historicism seems—consciously or otherwise—to have been what was widely attempted; and it is, in this area, that one may understand something of Marx's belated centrality. Invert Hegel's hierarchy of spiritual and physical; or delete Hegel's 'spirit' and substitute mechanism; retain Hegel's prophetic component but give it more ample orchestration by appeal to the French precedent of world-wide revolution; then, while the French system will subvert Hegel's metaphysic, the German will contribute to the French a sense of destiny and depth, an assurance of the superiority of becoming to being, and a knowledge of the forces of unconquerable motion.

This thesis is in no way original; but, with or without Marx's influence, the bringing into proximity of Hegelian and Saint-Simonian propositions could only be to endow them both with an urgency that, understood separately, they could not possess. An almost equivalent composition could be put together via the influence of Darwin—for French physics substitute English biology; fold in equal quantity of German *Geist*; add freshly ground crumbs of theosophy to taste and warm thoroughly in a moderate oven—but, though this combination was much resorted to in Germany, Holland, Wisconsin and elsewhere, though its contributions to architectural cuisine are not be be disputed, and even though Marx's favourite image of himself was the Darwin of sociology, this was apparently too particularized a strategy to lend itself to public establishment.

Nevertheless, Social Darwinism made its central contributions; and, as it dissipated something of the austerity of a physics-based world, corroborated Hegel's historicism, scarcely infringed his idealism, sustained his optimism, introduced the interesting ideas of natural selection and the survival of the fittest, and appeared to condone simply power, then we must recognize its contributions as being, in no way, to be despised.

And, at this stage, it is a temptation to say: And, hence the city of Sant'Elia—that city where static conceptions have vanished, where freedom has become the recognition of necessity, where machine has become spirit or spirit machine, and where the momentum of history has become the index to destiny. But, if it may be argued that there has here, in very impacted form, been presented a genealogy for the Futurist city, this is not a stage at which a halt can be called. For, as all the world knows, the Futurist city was no monument to the brotherhood of man; and thus, although we have cited it as the first of genuine activist utopian icons, it is also necessary to insert a qualification. There is the Futurist city as

Le Corbusier: Paris, Plan Voisin, 1925

proto-'modern'; there is the Futurist city as proto-Fascist; and there is the routine conviction that, because it may be the one, it cannot possibly be the other; but if there is here a problem which can only be related to the pervasive dogma of modern architecture's immaculate conception, then the time has now come to confront the *immaculata* at the moment of important delivery.

Futurism one might see as a sort of romantic front edge of Hegel; but, if the celebration of force is among its more important sustaining sentiments, this also allows us to insert it into an historical frame. Nietzsche's 'The human being who has become *free*–and how much more the *spirit* who has become free–spits on the contemptible type of well-being dreamed of by shopkeepers, Christians, cows, women, Englishmen, and other democrats; the free man is a *warrior*.'[20] bears an uncanny resemblance to Marinetti's 'We will glorify war–the only hygiene of the world–militarism, patriotism, the destructive gesture of anarchy, the beautiful ideas which kill, and the scorn of woman[21], and, after 1914-18, it was impossible that such sentiments could posture as avant garde, as other than retrospective. 'After that violent eruption,' says Walter Gropius, 'every thinking man felt the necessity for an intellectual change of front'[22]; but, if after World War I, the Futurist programme rapidly demonstrated its intrinsic atavism, then, as the *ville radieuse* came to be formulated–except for the absence of nationalism and related phallic fantasies–the basic components seem to have been much the same.

L'esprit nouveau and the *dynamisme des temps modernes* are again the romantic front edge of a de-spiritualized Hegel; and, via an appeal to Saint-Simonian 'science' ('demonstrations independent of the human will'), then, as the most pellucid 'moment' of the twentieth century utopia developed intensity, it became indeed possible for the architect to feel himself an undefiled creature. For, not only could he suppose himself to have shed his cultural wardrobe; but, to repeat the words of Finsterlin, he was even about to shed that constraining 'ether mantle' which, hitherto, had enveloped him 'like a skin'.

For present purposes, we see no reason to make a differentiation between the *ville radieuse* and *Zeilenbau city*, between Plan Voisin and Karlsruhe-Dammarstock; but, as we look back at the intellectual pedigree we have constructed for these, though convinced of its general correctness, we are also perturbed by its inadequacy. There is an abundance of ideas that are in themselves volatile; but one might still be obliged to recognize that, without the threat of all-consuming crisis (the equivalent of the threat of revolution), their mythical potency is much less than complete.

The utopia of the nineteen-twenties was born under a strange astrological combination: on the one hand Oswald Spengler, on the other, H. G. Wells; on the one side, eschatological prediction, the irreversible decline of the West, on the other the millennialistic future; and it is here that one may be concerned not so much with ideas as with ingrained, scarcely conscious habit.

If we have suggested an Hebraic thing—the promise of the messianic kingdom—and then its Christian version, if we have tried to discriminate this virulent thing, platonized in the Renaissance and secularized in the eighteenth century, then one could also be disposed to recognize the nineteenth century career of this secular residuum which, as it lost little of its virulence, now emerged from the political sphere to enter the aesthetic. It is a case of a metaphor of the good society thought of, quite literally, as becoming the thing itself, of myth become prescription and of prescription endorsed by the threat of Either:Or. A choice of utopia or else, the urbanistic vision of the nineteen-twenties is propounded in terms of the moral or biological problem of salvation; and building holds the key. 'The machinery of society, profoundly out of gear, oscillates between an amelioration, of historical importance, and a catastrophe'.[23]

Such was the essential backdrop and it is against this blinding light that there ultimately might be placed the whole extraordinary orchestration of German 'history' and French 'science', of spiritual explosiveness and mechanical coolness, of inevitability and observation, of people and progress. It was a light which generated energy and which, as it became compounded with the gentler forces of a liberal tradition and the romantic directives of a fledgling avant gardism, contributed to modern architecture the velocity of a projectile, enabling it to enter the twentieth century like some apocalyptic discharge of a newly invented shot gun; and, even though faded, this continues to be the light which still conditions any 'serious' endeavour connected with the 'structure' or the well being of society. But, however once vivid, it must finally be recognized that this is also a light which permits only a restrictive and monocular vision and it is therefore from the bias of normal optics than we must recognize and can speak of utopia's decline and fall.

After the Millennium

Whenever the utopia disappears, history ceases to be a process leading to an ultimate end. The frame of reference according to which we evaluate facts vanishes and we are left with a series of events all equal as far as their inner significance is concerned.
KARL MANNHEIM

Come to our well run desert
Where anguish arrives by cable
And the deadly sins may be bought in tins
With instructions on the label.
W. H. AUDEN

The parousia of modern architecture. A bundle of eschatological fantasies about imminent and apocalyptic catastrophe combined with still others about instant millennium. Crisis: the threat of damnation, the hope of salvation. Irresistible change which still requires human cooperation. The new architecture and urbanism as emblems of the New Jerusalem. The corruptions of high culture. The bonfire of vanities. Self-transcendence towards a form of collectivized freedom. The architect, repossessed of virtue and fortified by the equivalent of religious experience, may now revert to his primal innocence.

This is to caricature, though not seriously to distort a complex of sentiments often lying just beneath the threshold of consciousness, which have been crucial in forming the conscience of the modern movement.

Robert Lugar: double cottage, 1805, elevation and plan

Make me a cottage in the vale, she said,
Where I may mourn and pray.
Yet pull not down my palace towers, that are
So lightly, beautifully built;
Perchance I may return with others there
When I have purged my guilt.

The sentiments which Tennyson in *The Palace of Art* (1832-42) attributed to his soul were still, more or less, representative of the modern architect in the twenties and it is often difficult to dispute their abstemiousness and moral dignity. But, if 'a cottage in the vale' (a *cottage ornée* no doubt) can be sharply devalued as a symbol of innocence, so can other things also; and when, in the late nineteen-forties, modern architecture became established and institutionalized the image of the modern city necessarily suffered. Modern architecture had certainly arrived but the New Jerusalem was not exactly a going concern; and, slowly it began to appear that something had gone wrong. Modern architecture had not, *ipso facto*, resulted in a better world; and, as utopian fantasies correspondingly contracted, so, from the blurring of critical target, there ensued a certain aimlessness which it is probably true to say has afflicted the architect ever since. Could he any longer conceive himself to be the protagonist of a new integration of culture? Must he so conceive himself? And, if so, how?

Now the extent to which these questions were consciously asked was probably never large; but, all the same, their implicit presence could only create a divergence of interest revolving around the evaluation of the urban models of the twenties. Thus, on the one hand, the *ville radieuse* could be seen as a frightening false promise; but, on the other, it was still possible for a somewhat too assertive optimism to survive— and this by interpreting the Corbusian city as no more than a launching pad for the elaboration and perfection of the technocratically and scientifically inspired city of the future. Thus, on the one hand, an overtly backward look and, on the other, an ostensible look forward; and thus the cult of townscape and the cult of science fiction.

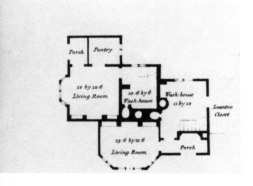

Townscape, a cult of English villages, Italian hill towns and North African casbahs, was, above all else, a matter of felicitous happenings and anonymous architecture; and, of course it made its first appearance well before the issues just suggested rose to the surface. Indeed, in the pages of *The Architectural Review*, even in the early nineteen-thirties, one can detect the uncoordinated presence of all its later ingredients. A perhaps wholly English taste for topography; a surely Bauhaus-inspired taste for the pregnant object of mass production—the hitherto unnoticed Victorian manhole, etc; a feeling for paint, the texture of decay, eighteenth century folly and nineteenth century graphics; representative titles of these early days include: *The Seeing Eye or How to Like Everything*; *Eyes and Ears in East Anglia—a schoolboy's holiday tour by Archibald Angus aged 14½*; *The Native Style*; *Warmth in the West*; *A Cubist Folk Art*; and, most significantly, two apparently crucial articles by Amédée Ozenfant who, in *Colour in the Town* (1937), states with obvious reference:

Leave it to the H. G. Wells of architecture to trace the outline of ideal towns, to sketch a hypothetical Paris or London of the year 3000. Let us accept the present, the actual condition of the English capital! Her past, her present and her immediate future. I would speak of what is immediately realizable.

At first startling, on reflection, the presence of Ozenfant in this collection ceases to be so. For this was the period of his brief domicile in London; and it would seem that, during this time, he was led to resume—though with less passionate intensity—that process of bringing

Gordon Cullen: townscape studies, 1961

right
publicity

below
Salisbury, Poultry Cross

far right above
pedestrian precinct

far right below
Looe, a proposal

into prominence hitherto undiscriminated aspects of vernacular or folk culture or mass production which he and Le Corbusier had practised some fifteen years earlier. Involving attitudes derived from the repertory of Synthetic Cubism and a Surrealist notion of the *object trouvé*, what Ozenfant might be felt to have provided was a criticism of London from the point of view of specifics, a criticism somewhat analogous to Le Corbusier's involvement with a specific rather than an ideal Paris—with a Paris of studio windows, the foyers of Métro stations, random rubble party walls and generally emotive accidents, an empirical Paris which Le Corbusier so often quoted in his buildings but never in his urbanistic proposals.

Ozenfant's two articles belong to the incunabula of townscape and are of far more than simply period interest. But, if it would seem that for a time the possibility was open of seeing the townscape idea as affiliated to Cubist and post-Cubist tradition, this was an opening which World War II, involving a devaluation of things French, tended to minimize. For there was always available the attractive and more comprehensible alternative of proclaiming the enduring significance of an indigenous style of vision. In other words, townscape could readily be interpreted as a derivative of the late eighteenth century Picturesque; and, as it implicated all that love of disorder, cultivation of the individual, distaste for the rational, passion for the various, pleasure in the idiosyncratic and suspicion of the generalized which may, sometimes, be supposed to distinguish the architectural tradition of the United Kingdom, so (almost

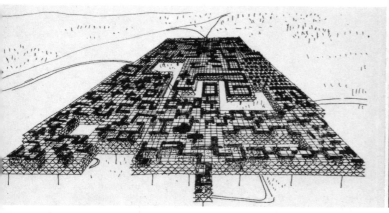

above
Yona Friedman: the spatial city, 1961

above right
Tatsuhiko Nakajima and GAUS:
Kibogaoka Youth Castel, c. 1971

below
NER Group, USSR: city project,
Moscow, 1967

like Edmund Burke's political polemic of the 1790s) it was enabled to thrive.

But, in application, townscape was surely less defensible than it was as an idea. It involved a highly interesting theory of the 'accident'– (its model was surely Serlio's popular and Comic Scene rather than the aristocratic and Tragic Scene which utopia had consistently employed) but, in practice, townscape seems to have lacked any ideal referent for the always engaging 'accidents' which it sought to promote; and, as a result, its tendency has been to provide sensation without plan, to appeal to the eye and not to the mind and, while usefully sponsoring a perceptual world, to devalue a world of concepts.

It may be argued that these limitations are not intrinsic to the approach, that townscape can be detached from what too early became an undue preoccupation with beer and yachting; but, meanwhile, it should be enough to stipulate its importance as a doctrine. Scarcely dependent upon Camillo Sitte, as is sometimes erroneously supposed, much of present-day activity is incomprehensible unless we are prepared to recognize the ramifications of townscape's influence. Beyond its basic visuals townscape has become the point of reference for a number of related arguments. Thus, it has been given a sociological and economic credibility by Jane Jacobs; it has been given rational gloss by the allegedly scientific notational systems of Kevin Lynch; and, if advocacy planning and do-it-yourself are inconceivable without the influence of townscape, so equally are Pop-inspired appraisals of the

Arato Isozaki: space city project, collage, 1960

Strip at Las Vegas and enthusiasm for the phenomenon of Disney World.

Like townscape, what we have chosen to call science fiction also antedates the collapse of modern architecture's millennialistic idea. But, if it is to be related to Futurist and Expressionist precedent, it is also to be seen as, in some sense, a revival. Science fiction identifies itself with mega-buildings, lightweight throwaways, plug-in variability, over-city grids—ironing-board over Stockholm, waffle-iron over Düsseldorf— linear cities, integration of buildings with transport, movement systems and tubes. It displays a preference for process and hyper-rationalization, for crude facts as found, an obsession with the spirit of the times. Its vocabulary displays a conversance with computer technology; and,

Cumbernauld town centre, model of
early design

Cumbernauld, residential area

if the *ville radieuse* carried with it the implication of a future, science
fiction pushes this conviction even further.

To one extent, of course, science fiction is modern architecture with
all its old style presumptions as to the rational determination of building
surviving intact, even though a little hysterically over stipulated. That
is: in so far as methodology, systems analysis and parametric design are
elevated to be important pursuits, science fiction may present itself as
an academicized version of what modern architecture was, anciently,
supposed to be. But science fiction, like old-fashioned modern architecture, has, also a less rigorous more poetic face. This is the familiar
involvement with images conceived to illustrate science and then their
advertisement as proofs of the designer's all-relevant objectivity.

But science fiction, which may thus be either pure or Pop, in spite
of all its prophetic gestures, may also be thought of as the reverse of
anything revolutionary. The search for system, after all, is very like the
old academic thing–platonic certainty in brave new disguise; while
even elaborate concern for the future may also be seen as regressive and
status quo-ist. In fact, science fiction, in some of its more free forms,
suffers from some of the same defects as the Futurism of which it is the
unconsciously ironical revival. Which is to say: that for all its action-
directed posture, inherently, it is almost unbelievably passive; that
rather than protest, it largely involves endorsement of what is supposed
to be endemic; that, rather than being conscious of morals, it is apt to
be success-oriented; and that, like the original Futurists, some of its
devotees are perfectly willing, if useful (because such is cultural relativism), to describe black as being white.

An attitude to Futurism has already here been divulged, the celebration of *force majeure*, a nationalist and essentially pre-1914 manifes-
tation; and, to this we might add Kenneth Burke's observation that the
Futurist propensity was to make of an abuse a virtue. To the protest: the
streets are noisy, there was the characteristic reply, we prefer it that way;
and, to the proposition: the drains smell, there was the entirely predictable response, well we like stink.[1] But, all this apart, in Futurism, there
still remains the Marinetti-Mussolini *degringolade*;[2] and, without wishing
obsessively to insist upon this, it can only be conceded that it does
qualify present judgements.

In any case, the results of science fiction, whether systemic or neo-
Futurist, usually suffer from the same conditions which plague the *ville
radieuse*–disregard for context, distrust of the social continuum, the use
of symbolic utopian models for literal purposes, the assumption that the
existing city will be made to go away; and, if the *ville radieuse* is now
supposed to be evil, productive of trauma and disorientation, it is not
easy to see how science fiction, which would seem to compound the
ills, is in any position to alleviate the problem.

Nevertheless, an indebtedness to science fiction may still be proclaimed; and, if we are now provided with two models which Françoise

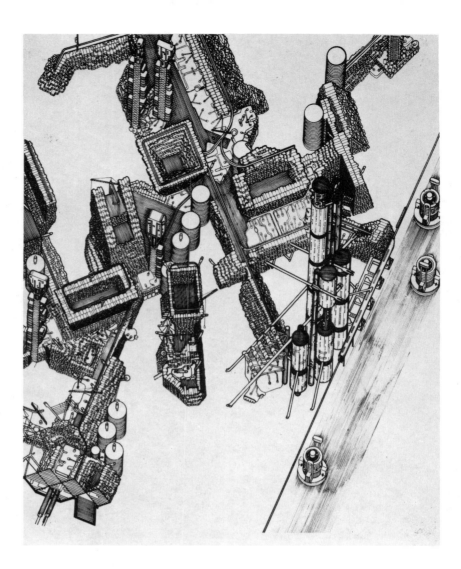

Archigram: plug-in city, 1964

Choay might designate *culturalist* and *progressivist*,[3] we might reasonably anticipate their cross-breeding–a process which both parties may be at pains to deny. But, possible denials apart, the offspring are evident; and in such an example as Cumbernauld, for instance, a great clash of townscape and neo-Futurism is, perhaps inadvertently, the prevailing idea. We live in townscape and, after a trek, we shop in Futurism; and, as we migrate between the 'relative' and the 'rational', between fantasies of what was and what is to be, then, receiving as we do an elementary lesson in philosophy and its variants, no doubt we can scarcely fail but be edified.

And of interest in the same respect is the work of Archigram and Team X. Judging by the bulk of its proposals for urban application, Archigram would seem to be making *picturesque images of the future*. For, all of the unplanned randomness, the happy jerkiness, the obviously high-pitched tonality, the aggressive syncopation, all of the famous ingredients of Englishness in action are now given a space-age gloss.

Anything might here happen: the death of architecture, non-building, Andy Warhol bug-eyed monsters, immediacy of feeling for life, instant nomadism, the wished-for end of all repression. We are presented with townscape in a space-suit; but whereas the idiosyncrasies of the townscape images are supposedly attributable to the pressures of context, the Archigram images are generally presented in an ideal void which, for all intents and purposes is the same void as that in which the urban model of *c*. 1930 is located.

But, if Archigram might represent an engagingly incidental and accidental fusion of the retrospective and the prospective models, Team X, by reason of its loose organization and diversity of manifestations, is less easy to characterize. Team X found the ideality and the taste for generality of classic modern architecture to be largely without meaning; but, if it denounced the Athens Charter and the related pronouncements of CIAM as having become irrelevant, it would seem that (perhaps by intention), it has failed to develop any body of theory of equivalent coherence. For Team X bears the weight of what it supposes to be the apostolic succession; and, though it often endeavours to compensate for this elevated predicament by insubstantial graphics and verbal infantilism, though its members have been careful not to trap themselves in a web of *ex cathedra* statements, one senses in their invariably cautious performance the consciousness of almost ecclesiastical responsibility. It has been stated (Bakema) that Team X would replace the isolated building and building programme with the overlapping of buildings and programmes, that it would replace functional organization with 'human association'[4] and, a more recent move, that for imposition it would substitute participation;[5] but, admirable though all these proposals are (and who would wish to disagree with such

below
Alison and Peter Smithson: layout for a provincial market town with established local market, 1967

below right
Candilis, Josic and Woods: project for Toulouse-le-Mirail, 1961

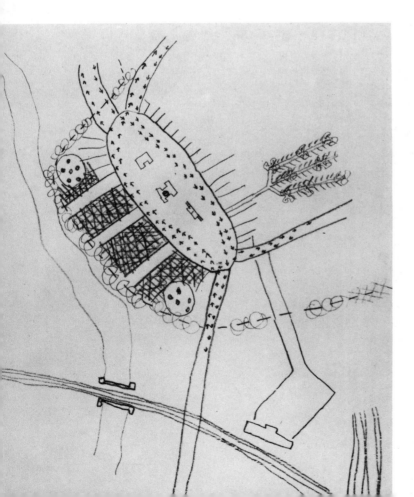

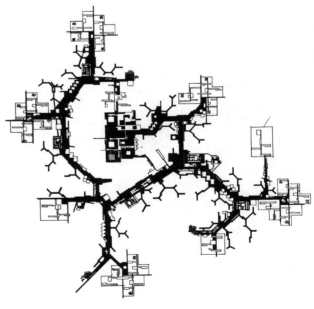

Superstudio: landscape with figures, c.1970

The mid-western prairie

wholesome generalities), the product is not, exactly, distinguishable. And thus Team X alternates between systems building and simulated villages, between growth fantasies and townscape tune up.[6]

Now, evidently, the various uneasy fusions of science fiction and townscape—all claiming to be libertarian and non-repressive—must signify a considerable investment of emotional capital; but, before proposing the question: Is it worth it? it now becomes necessary to recognise the latest representatives (the ultimate logical derivatives?) of the two models. At which stage the utopia of Superstudio and the 'symbolic American utopia' which Robert Venturi has professed to discover in Disney World[7] may conveniently exhibit the extremes to which the two critiques of the *ville radieuse* have (for the moment?) reduced themselves.

Notoriously, the exigencies of freedom (no imposition of authority) will support the most contradictory positions; and, ostensibly, this is what we here find. The utopia of Superstudio—the world as abstract Cartesian grid—demands a final emancipation from the tyranny of objects, and the alleged utopia of Disney World—an essentially naturalistic situation—suggests that, rather than any problem, objects are a relief; but, if the one proposes the supersession of the object while the

Ithaca, New York, State Street, 1869

Disney World, Florida, Main Street

other results in its fatal devaluation, they are, of course, both alike in insisting on the possibilities of apparently immediate gratification.

And to insist on the ideal shared. For Superstudio:

You can be where you like taking with you the tribe or family.
There's no need for shelters, since the climatic conditions and the body mechanisms of thermo-regulation have been modified to guarantee total comfort.
At the most we can play at making shelter, or rather at the home, at architecture.
All you have to do is to stop and connect a plug: the desired micro-climate is immediately created (temperature, humidity, etc.); you plug in to the network of information, you switch on the food and water blenders...[8]

And thus, with certain qualifications, also for Disney World.

But, when Superstudio continues that, in the ideal society:

There will be no further need for cities or castles. No further need for roads or squares. Every point will be the same as any other (excluding a few deserts or mountains which are in no wise inhabitable).[9]

it is then, evidently, that the two visions again part company. For freedom in Florence and freedom in Dubuque, apparently, bear different faces; and it is precisely such a situation as Superstudio projects that Disney World grew up to alleviate. It is not a question that, in fact, in Iowa there are no castles or squares; but it *is* a matter that the absence of these items may (sometimes) be felt as deprivation, a matter that, where the 'ideal' Cartesian grid has long been a fact of life, some relief may (occasionally) be sought which has guaranteed the popular success of Disney World.

So, to a degree, since they are linked in a chain of cause and effect, the two visions are still complementary. Superstudio, in the interests of a non-oppressive egalitarianism, would systematically eradicate all existing variety in favour of an ideally uniform stage (it is probably called a plateau) for spontaneous happening; and, if Disney World proceeds from a commercial exploitation of the needs of just such a stage, then, perhaps, the only outstanding difference concerns the quality of the action or its source of origin.

In other words, the only outstanding difference relates to a conception of society, though, even here, relationships are closer than might at first be supposed. And thus, while Superstudio envisions the withering away of the state, Disney World is the product of a social situation where the evidence of the public realm was never very highly assertive. Simply, Superstudio proposes 'the elimination of the formal structures of power'; while Disney World is an attempt to furnish the resultant vacuum.

The problem may, therefore, ultimately reduce itself to one of style; to the question of what is acceptable furniture; to the question: may human bodies, preferably naked and surrounded by minimum apparatus, be construed as acceptable furniture, or are we obliged to assume that a little more is required? Which is also the question as to whether we make our furniture ourselves or order it from Grand Rapids. For, in both cases, the furniture is something which simply floats above an operative infra-structure and presents itself as 'real' or 'illusory' according to taste. In both cases we are in dream worlds exhibiting different styles of sophistication—with the implicit proviso that, for Superstudio, there is somehow an intrinsic connection between the infra-structure and what is dependent upon it. Given the 'correct' infra-structure:

We'll keep silence to listen to our bodies.
We'll watch ourselves living.
The mind will fall back on itself to read its own history.
We'll play wonderful games of ability and love.
We'll talk a lot, to ourselves and to everybody.
Life will be the only environmental art.[10]

Now the objectives of Walt Disney Enterprises are, surely, never to be formulated in exactly this manner. 'Buy homemade cookies from a turn of the century mercenary grandma on Main Street; visit the air conditioned Cinderella's Castle by elevator' (who needs Chambord?); in Adventureland 'come face to face with a gigantic python, be menaced by trumpeting African elephants;... pass under the plunging, thundering Albert Schweitzer Falls;'[11] in Tomorrowland, in seven minutes, ride an earthbound rocket to the moon; and, eventually, exercise the exotic emotions elicited by cheap air travel—Isfahan, Bangkok, Tahiti—in the hotels corresponding to these themes.

So much is a composite picture of the above-ground delights of Disney World where several hundred acres of mostly fibre glass fantasy rest upon an unseen technological substructure without earthly parallel, where, with easy access and accommodating all the vast priorities of change, are contained all the required services—vacuum garbage systems, electrical circuitry, sewage lines, complete supply tractor traffic routes and total behind (or below) the scenes access for the costumed employees

Paris, grand staircase of the Opéra

who fuel the various theatres of illusion above; and it should be evident that the correct analogy is that of the New York skyscraper: on the 65th floor is the Rainbow Room where the consumption of Transcendentalist cocktails is the order of the day and then, way, way beneath (out of sight but not out of mind) is the pragmatic sub-basement which facilitates both the upstairs afflatus and public euphoria. In both cases the two worlds of illusion and fact, of publicity and privacy are insulated. Inter-dependent but separate, they may possibly be equal, but, in no way, are they to be integrated; and, if the example of Second Empire Paris may here be quoted, what we have in each case is the underworld of Haussmann's sewers and the superworld of Garnier's Opéra.

To the strict moralist–though there may not be many left–there is in these conditions of apparent schism something which must be very profoundly wrong; but, if it will seem to him that here technology and art are simultaneously abused, it might still be desirable for this notoriously intolerant personage to suppress his initial reactions. For, if it is almost certain that the strict moralist, whose temperament is after all a little early Christian, will wish to assign primary value only to the technological catacombs, then, although his point of view is to be understood, this attribution of authenticity only to the props of illusion must, in the end, be considered self-defeating. For, given the rifting of 'reality' and 'fantasy', it is a question of what sponsors what: Do the sewers validate the Opéra or does the Opéra validate the sewers; which has priority, the servant or the served?

Modern architecture, and Superstudio following its general lead, has always wished to abolish this gross distinction, or even to obliterate the question; but if, in seeking to do so, it has, perhaps inadvertently, too much accepted the Marxian distinction of 'structure' and 'superstructure' assigning importance and significance only to the first, then the results of a total failure to consider the problem are not too hard to describe.

Paris, a visit to the sewers, from *Le Magasin Pittoresque*

'Disney World is nearer to what people really want than what architects have ever given them'.[12] The judgement is Robert Venturi's; and, whether it is correct or not (because who really knows?), it must be allowed at least to embody an important half truth. So Disney World is justifiably popular; and, if we judge it for what it is, this should surely be enough. But when a derivative of townscape has been annexed by the entertainment industry and is then polemically represented as a utopia and as 'a symbolic American utopia' then wholly different critical standards become activated; and, if the inter-dependence of kitsch and government is nothing new, then surely (and however Fauve-Dada we may wish to be) this does not necessarily call for the inversion of all serious judgements of value.

Disney World deals with the crude and the obvious; and this is both its virtue and limitation. Its images are not complex; and, thus, Disney

World's Main Street is not so much an idealization of the real thing as it is a filtering and packaging operation, involving the elimination of un-pleasantness, of tragedy, of time and of blemish.

But the real Main Street, the authentic nineteenth century thing is neither so facile nor so felicitous. It registers, instead, an optimistic desperation. The Greek temple, the false Victorian façade, the Palladian portico, the unused Opera-House, the courthouse sanctioned by the glamour of Napoleon III's Paris, the conspicuous monument to the Civil War or to the Fearless Fireman,[13] these are the evidence of almost frenzied effort, via the movingly ingenuous reconstitution of stable cultural images, to provide stability in an unstable scene, to convert frontier flux into established community. Main Street was never very pretty nor, probably, ever very prosperous; but it was a posture towards the world involving both independence and enterprise and it was never lacking in a rawness of pathetic dignity. Its clumsy, would-be metro-politan veneers are the indications of a certain stoicism of mood, of a sort of embittered flamboyance, which acquires its final dignity from its essential lack of success. That is, while Main Street was an often grand attempt to dissimulate real hardship and deprivation—an attempt which could only fail, one may still sometimes, even in its physical inadequacy, discern the implicit grandeur of its moral impulse.

In other words, the real Main Street, about which there may often be something a little sardonic, is an exhibition of a reserved and scarcely agreeable reality, of a reality which engages speculative curiosity, which stimulates the imagination and which, for its understanding, insists upon the expenditure of mental energy. In the real Main Street there is, inevitably, a two-way commerce between the observer and the observed; but the Disney World version can scarcely allow for any such risky business. The Disney World version cannot seriously emulate its enigmatic original. A machine for the production of euphoria, it can only leave the imagination unprovoked and the capacity for speculation unstimulated; and, while it might be argued that the nausea produced by over-exposure to sugar coating and eternally fixed smiles might guarantee a certain genuine and unpleasant emotional response, then there is surely some question (sado-masochism notwithstanding) as to whether such a traumatic experience is really necessary.

But if, implicitly, we have assigned to Billy Graham the role of Archbishop of Canterbury (it could never be Pope) of Disney World, then we are still constrained to ask: How about Superstudio; Super-studio which moves upon Italianate levels of cosmopolitan intelligence and which, from a basis of bourgeois neo-Marxism, propounds (we believe correctly) the unavoidable *dénouement* of science fiction? And what to reply? To say that, in Superstudio, we discern a little too much of the *bella figura* syndrome, that we are not unobservant of an insidiously neo-Fascist content? We do not suppose these to be adequate responses. For Superstudio writes of: 'Design, become perfect and rational, (which)

Ithaca, New York, State Street, 1869

proceeds to synthesize different realities by syncretism...Thus designing coincides more and more with existence: no longer existence under the protection of design objects, but existence as design'.[14] And what to say about this? That such poetry may seduce but can seldom convince; that insistence upon total freedom is to deny the small approximate freedoms which are all that, historically, have been available and are probably all that we can ever anticipate?[15] Perhaps; and certainly, if Superstudio seems to envisage the future 'city' as a continuous Wood-stock festival for the benefit of 'all' (meaning a highly restricted elite), a Woodstock without garbage, then as we examine Superstudio's images, we cannot exactly rid ourselves of an impression. For are we not to suppose—indeed can we do other—that these are the products of an enlightened gesture on the part of the editor of *Playboy* magazine? Certainly there is here no 'oppression'; and if the libido rides unchecked, we might even imagine that these are among the results of an invitation to Herbert Marcuse to prepare a special issue of Hugh Hefner's publi-cation...so far as we can see a kitsch not unequivalent to the kitsch of Disney World.

But, if a pun may be admitted and we might believe that Super-studio and Disney World are only alternative versions of the kitsch of death, then, if one is to be relegated to the status of the reader of a 'heavy' skin magazine or obliged to find hope only in false pieties, the time has surely come to recognize that any argument (and particularly a partisan argument) if pursued to its logical termination can only be self-destructive. Thus we have cited Disney World and the images of Superstudio, not for their intrinsic virtues and vices, but rather as the logical extensions of two points of view which, in themselves, may both be valuable; but the presumption here inferred that only the middle ground of an argument is of use, that its extremities are likely always to be absurd, is now positively introduced, not from any passion for compromise, but as an intuition which might assist some kind of alert and workable *détente*.

Thus far we have characterized modern architecture as, first, a bout with destiny and then as a morning-after nausea which, for relief, made use of at least two time-tested recipes: an analgesic pain remover, or more of the same; but, if we have further suggested that sometimes these remedies were administered simultaneously and sometimes in excess, the question as to whether all this activity was really worth-while cannot any longer be postponed.

We have surveyed a scene which, fundamentally, endorses retrospective attitudes, exploiting known and, perhaps, popular references; we have also witnessed an extension of the prospective and future-oriented aspects of modern architecture, involving techno-scientific resources and, in the end, the dematerialized and oppression-free utopian state; but then one is also compelled to recognize that in neither of these two traditions has there emerged an urbanistic statement capable of offsetting that of early modern architecture. Nor have attempts to reconcile this duality of approach been, so far, very successful; and, because any such attempts have been too far removed from effective usage or too hesitant and various to admit of coherent interpretation, the problem presented by early modern architecture—the fantasy of the comprehensive city of deliverance, propounded as poetry and read as prescription, institutionalized in grotesque and cut-rate form—still remains, to become every day more impossible to ignore. And the problem remains what to do?

Given the recognition that utopian models will founder in the cultural relativism which, for better or worse, immerses us, it would seem only reasonable to approach such models with the greatest circumspection; given the inherent dangers and debilitations of any institutionalized *status quo*—and particularly a *status quo ante* (more of Levittown, more of Wimbledon, even more of Urbino and Chipping Camden)—it would also seem that neither simple 'give them what they want' nor unmodified townscape are equipped with sufficient conviction to provide more than partial answers; and, such being the case, it becomes necessary to conceive of a strategy which might, one hopes, and without disaster, accommodate the ideal and which might plausibly, and without devaluation, respond to what we believe the real to be.

In a recent book, *The Art of Memory*,[16] Frances Yates speaks of Gothic cathedrals as mnemonic devices. The bibles and the encyclopedias of both the illiterate and the literate, these buildings were intended to articulate thought by assisting recollection; and, to the degree that they

acted as Scholastic classroom aids, it becomes possible to refer to them as
having been *theatres of memory*. And the designation is a useful one,
because if today we are only too apt to think of buildings as necessarily
prophetic, such an alternative mode of thinking may serve to correct
our unduly prejudiced naïveté. The building as *a theatre of prophecy*, the
building as *a theatre of memory*—if we are able to conceive of the building
as the one, we must, inherently, be able also to conceive of it as the other;
and, while recognizing that, without benefit of academic theory, this is
the way in which we habitually *do* interpret buildings, we might further
observe that this memory-prophecy theatre distinction could well be
carried over into the urbanistic field.

Of course, having said just so much and no more, it goes almost
without saying that exponents of the city as prophecy theatre would be
likely to be thought of as radicals while exponents of the city as memory
theatre would, almost certainly be described as conservatives; but, if
there might be some degree of truth in such assumption, it must also be
established that block notions of this kind are not really very useful. The
mass of mankind is likely to be, at any one time, both conservative and
radical, to be preoccupied with the familiar and diverted by the unexpected; and, if we all of us both live in the past and hope for the future (the
present being no more than an episode in time), it would seem reasonable
that we should accept this condition. For, if without prophecy there is
no hope, then, without memory there can be no communication.

Obvious, trite and sententious though this may be, it was—happily
or unhappily—an aspect of the human mind which the early proponents
of modern architecture were able to overlook—happily for them,
unhappily for us. But, if without such distinctly perfunctory psychology,
'the new way of building' could never have come into being, there
cannot any longer be excuse for the failure to recognize the complementary relationship which is fundamental to the processes of anticipation
and retrospection. For these are inter-dependent activities; and since,
quite literally, we cannot perform without exercising them both, no
attempt to suppress either in the interests of the other can ever be
protractedly successful. We may receive strength from the novelty of
prophetic declamation; but the degree of this potency must be strictly
related to the known, perhaps mundane and, necessarily, memory-laden
context from which it emerges.

Which almost completes a phase of argument; and, since it is an
argument which here must be left open, for present purposes it might
conveniently be terminated in the form of three questions:
Why should we be *obliged* to prefer a nostalgia for the future to that
for the past?
Could not the model city which we carry in our minds allow for our
known psychological constitution?
Could not this ideal city, at one and the same time, behave, quite explicitly,
as both a theatre of prophecy *and* a theatre of memory?

Crisis of the Object: Predicament of Texture

Cities force growth and make men talkative and entertaining *but* they make men artificial.
RALPH WALDO EMERSON

I think that our governments will remain virtuous as long as they are chiefly agricultural.
THOMAS JEFFERSON

But . . . how can man withdraw himself from the fields?Where will he go, since the earth is one huge unbounded field? Quite simple; he will mark off a portion of this field by means of walls, which set up an enclosed finite space over against amorphous, limitless space . . . For in truth the most accurate definition of the *urbs* and the *polis* is very like the comic definition of a cannon. You take a hole, wrap some steel wire tightly around it, and that's your cannon. So the *urbs* or *polis* starts by being an empty space . . . and all the rest is just a means of fixing that empty space, of limiting its outlines . . . The square . . . This lesser rebellious field which secedes from the limitless one, and keeps to itself, is a space *sui generis* of the most novel kind in which man frees himself from the community of the plant and the animal . . . and creates an enclosure apart which is purely human, a civil space.
JOSÉ ORTEGA Y GASSET

In intention the modern city was to be a fitting home for the noble savage. A being so aboriginally pure necessitated a domicile of equivalent purity; and, if way back the noble savage had emerged from the trees, then, if his will-transcending innocence was to be preserved, his virtues maintained intact, it was back into the trees that he must be returned.

One might imagine that such an argument was the ultimate psychological rationale of the *ville radieuse* or *Zeilenbau city*, a city which, in its complete projection, was almost literally imagined as becoming non-existent. Immediately necessary buildings appear, so far as possible, as delicate and unassertive intrusions into the natural continuum; buildings raised above the ground provide as little contact as possible with the potentially reclaimable earth; and, while there ensues a freedom-releasing qualification of gravity, we are perhaps also encouraged to recognize a commentary upon the dangers of prolonged exposure to any conspicuous artifact.

The projected modern city, in this way, may be seen as a transitional piece, a proposal which eventually, it is hoped, may lead to the re-establishment of an unadulterated natural setting.

Sun, space, verdure: essential joys, through the four seasons stand the trees, friends of man. Great blocks of dwellings run through the town. What does it matter? They are behind the screen of trees. Nature is entered into the lease.[1]

Such was the vision of an ever-evolving return to nature, a return that was (and is) evidently felt to be so important that, whenever possible, demonstrations of this vision have insisted on their absolute detachment, symbolic and physical, from any aspects of existing context which has been, typically, envisaged as a contaminant, as something both morally and hygienically leprous. And thus Lewis Mumford on an illustration in his *Culture of Cities*:

Rear of a handsome facade in Edinburgh: barracks architecture facing a catwalk: typical indifference to rear views characteristic of scene painting. An architecture of fronts. Beautiful silks, costly perfumes, Elegance of mind and small pox. Out of sight, out of mind. Modern functional planning distinguishes itself from this purely visual conception of the plan, by dealing honestly and competently with every side, abolishing the gross distinction between front and rear, seen and obscene, and creating structures that are harmonious in every dimension.[2]

Paris, Place des Vosges (Place Royale).
From the Plan Turgot, 1739

Le Corbusier: Ville Radieuse, 1930

Which, allowing for a characteristically Mumfordian rhetoric, is all classically representative of the bias of the inter-war period. The prominent criteria are honesty and hygiene, the city of vested interest and impacted association is to disappear; and, in place of traditional subterfuge and imposition, there is to be introduced a visible and rational equality of parts—an equality which insists upon openness and is readily to be interpreted as both cause and effect of any condition of humane well-being.

Now, of course, the equation of the backyard with moral and physical insalubrity, which becomes the opposition of closure and openness and their investment with negative and positive qualities ('Elegance of mind and small pox'—as though the one automatically followed the other), could be illustrated from an abundance of other sources; and, in terms of that distinctively nineteenth century vision of the *danse macabre*, the human scarecrow in the cholera-infected courtyard, this style of agument should scarcely require reinforcement. Visually oriented architects and planners, preoccupied with the trophies and triumphs of culture, with the representation of the public realm and its public façades, had, for the most part, shamefully compromised not only the pleasurable possibilities but, worse than this, the essential sanitary bases of that more intimate world within which 'real' people, people as deserving aspects of concern, actually do exist. And, if this statement were to be augmented to say something about pragmatically callous capitalists then its general substance would not be radically transformed.

But, if such was the one-time negative and necessary criticism of traditional metropolis, then if an overview of nineteenth century Paris can be allowed to represent the evil, an overview of Amsterdam South may also be introduced to exhibit the initial conceptions of an alternative; and both illustrations derive from the accessible pages of Siegfried Giedion.[3]

The Hausmannesque situation, as witnessed by a bird or from a balloon, is so sufficiently comparable to the air photo of Berlagian Amsterdam as to need the minimum of comment. Both are subservient to the aesthetic of the French seventeenth century hunting forest with its *ronds-points* and *pattes-d'oie*; and, in being so, they both of them, by means of major arteries converging at a, hopefully, significant place, describe a triangular territory as subject for development or infill. But then it is here, with the infill, that resemblance ceases. For, if among the grandeurs and brutalities of Second Empire Paris, logical infill could be disregarded, if it could be reduced to the abstract volumetric status of trees in a garden by Le Nôtre, then in conscientious early twentieth century Holland such a highly casual universal matrix or 'texture' was, emphatically, not available. And, because of the French prototype, the result is a Dutch embarrassment. In Amsterdam a genuine attempt has been made to provide a more tolerable theatre of existence. Air, light, prospect, open space have all been made available; but, while one may sense that one is here on the threshold of the welfare state, one may still be overcome by the anomaly. The two big avenues, for all their ambitious protestation, are diffident and residual. They are lacking in the vulgar or the boring swagger and self-confidence of their Parisian prototypes. They are among the last

above
Cheltenham, rear view of Lansdown Terrace

below
Exeter, Barnfield Crescent

pathetic gestures to the notion of the street; and their carefully edited concessions to *De Stijl* or to Expressionism do not conceal their predicament. They have become no more than the conservatively insinuated props to a dying idea. For, in the argument of solid versus void they have become redundant; and their references to a vision of classical Paris now have nothing to say. Simply these avenues are disposable. In no way do their façades designate any effective frontier between public and private. They are evasive. And much more than the façades of eighteenth century

below
Amsterdam South, 1934

opposite above Paris, Boulevard Richard-Lenoir, 1861–3

opposite below Amsterdam South, c.1961

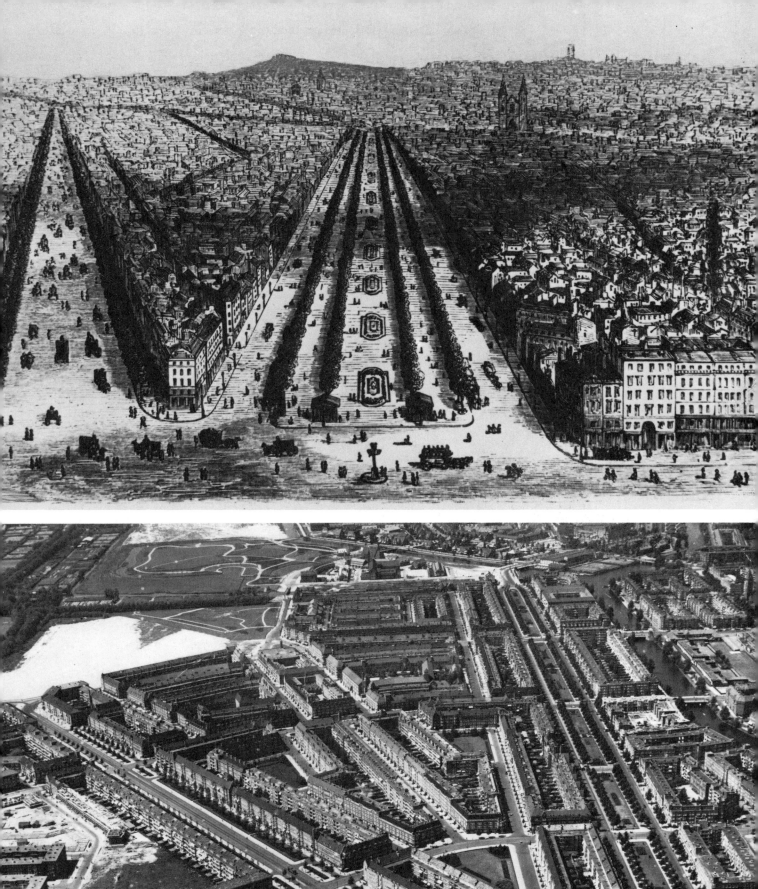

Edinburgh, they ineffectively conceal. For the important reality has now become what lies behind. The matrix of the city has become transformed from continuous solid to continuous void.

It goes without saying that both the failure and success of Amsterdam South, and of many comparable projects, could only activate the conscience; but, whatever may have been the doubts (the conscience is always more activated by failure than success), it probably remains true to say that logical scepticism was not able to digest the issue for at least some ten years. Which is to say that, until the late nineteen-twenties, the culturally obligatory street still dominated the scene and that, as a result, certain conclusions remained unapproachable.

In this sequence, the questions of who did what and precisely when and where are, for present purposes, irrelevant. The City of Three Million Inhabitants, miscellaneous Russian projects, Karlsruhe-Dammarstock, etc., all have their dates; and the assignment of priority or praise or blame is not here an issue. Simply the issue is that, by 1930, the disintegration of the street and of all highly organized public space seemed to have become inevitable; and for two major reasons: the new and rationalized form of housing and the new dictates of vehicular activity. For, if the configuration of housing now evolved from the inside out, from the logical needs of the individual residential unit, then it could no longer be subservient to external pressures; and, if external public space had become so functionally chaotic as to be without effective significance, then—in any case—there were no valid pressures which it could any longer exert.

Such were the apparently unfaultable deductions which underlay the establishment of the city of modern architecture; but, around these primary arguments, there was evidently the opportunity for a whole miscellany of secondary rationalizations to proliferate. And thus the new city could achieve further justification in terms of sport or of science, in terms of democracy or equality, in terms of history and absence of traditional *parti pris*, in terms of private automobiles and public transport, in terms of technology and socio-political crisis; and, like the idea of the city of modern architecture itself, in some form or another, almost all of these arguments are still with us.

And, of course, they are reinforced (though whether reinforcement is the correct word may be doubted) by others. 'A building is like a soap bubble. This bubble is perfect and harmonious if the breath has been evenly distributed from the inside. The exterior is the result of an interior.'[4] This debilitating half truth has proved to be one of Le Corbusier's more persuasive observations. That it never had very much to do with practice should be obvious; but, if it is an impeccable statement of academic theory relating to domed and vaulted structures, it is also a dictum which could only lend support to the notion of the building as preferably a free standing object in the round. Lewis Mumford intimates as much; but, if for Theo Van Doesburg and many others it was axiomatic that 'the new architecture will develop in an all sided plastic way,'[5]

Theo Van Doesburg: Counter-
construction, maison particulière, 1923

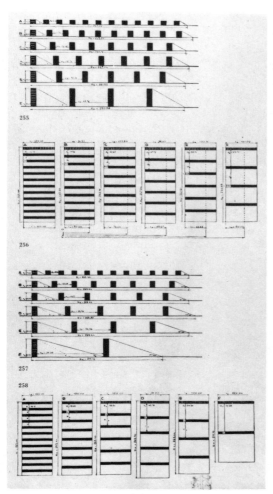

Walter Gropius: diagrams showing the
development of a rectangular site with
parallel rows of apartment blocks of
different heights, 1929

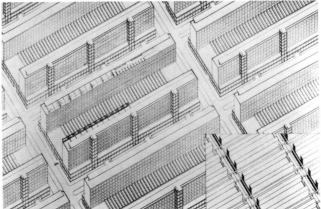

Ludwig Hilberseimer: project for
central Berlin, 1927

this placing of immensely high premia upon the building as 'interesting' and detached object (which still continues) must now be brought into conjunction with the simultaneously entertained proposition that the building (object?) must be made to go away ('Great blocks of dwellings run through the town. What does it matter? They are behind the screen of trees'). And, if we have here presented this situation in terms of a typically Corbusian self-contradiction, there is obvious and abundant reason to recognize that one is confronted with this same contradiction any, and every, day. Indeed, in modern architecture, the pride in objects and the wish to dissimulate pride in this pride, which is everywhere revealed, is something so extraordinary as to defeat all possibility of compassionate comment.

But modern architecture's object fixation (the object which is not an object) is our present concern only in so far as it involves the city, the city which was to become evaporated. For, in its present and unevaporated form, the city of modern architecture become a congeries of conspicuously disparate objects is quite as problematical as the traditional city which it has sought to replace.

Let us, first of all, consider the theoretical desideratum that the rational building is obliged to be an object and, then, let us attempt to place this proposition in conjunction with the evident suspicion that buildings, as man-made artefacts, enjoy a meretricious status, in some way, detrimental to an ultimate spiritual release. Let us further attempt to place this demand for the rational materialization of the object and this parallel need for its disintegration alongside the very obvious feeling that space is, in some way, more sublime than matter, that, while the affirmation of matter is inevitably gross, the affirmation of a spatial continuum can only facilitate the demands of freedom, nature and spirit. And then let us qualify what became a widespread tendency to space worship with

Le Corbusier: project for city centre of Saint-Dié, 1945, plan

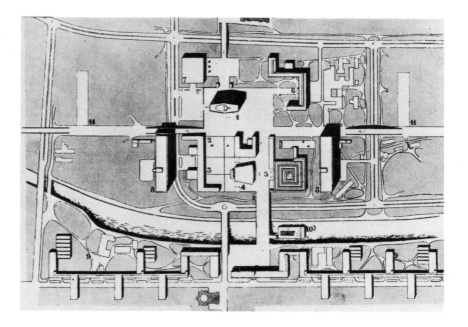

Le Corbusier: project for city centre of Saint-Dié, 1945, perspective

yet another prevalent supposition: that, if space is sublime, then limitless naturalistic space must be far more so than any abstracted and structured space; and, finally, let us upstage this whole implicit argument by introducing the notion that, in any case, space is far less important than time and that too much insistence—particularly upon delimited space—is likely to inhibit the unrolling of the future and the natural becoming of the 'universal society.'

Such are some of the ambivalences and fantasies which were, and still are, embedded in the city of modern architecture; but, though these could seem to add up to a cheerful and exhilarating prescription, as already noticed, even when realizations of this city, though pure, were only partial, doubts about it began very early to be entertained. Perhaps these were scarcely articulated doubts and whether they concerned the necessities of perception or the predicament of the public realm is difficult to determine; but, if, in the Athens Congress of 1933[6] CIAM had spelled out the ground rules for the new city, then by the mid-forties there could be no such dogmatic certainty. For neither the state nor the object had vanished away; and, in CIAM's *Heart of the City*[7] conference of 1947, lurking reservations as to their continuing validity began, indecisively, to surface. Indeed, a consideration of the 'city core', in itself, already indicates a certain hedging of bets and, possibly, the beginnings of a recognition that the ideal of indiscriminate neutrality or inconspicuous equality was hardly attainable or even desirable.

But, if a renewed interest in the possibilities of focus and hence of confluence seems, by this time, to have been developing, while the interest was there, the equipment to service it was lacking; and the problem presented by the revisionism of the late forties might best be typified and illustrated by Le Corbusier's plan for St. Dié, where modified standard elements of Athens Charter specification are loosely arranged so as to insinuate some notions of centrality and hierarchy, to simulate some version of 'town centre' or structured receptacle. And might it be said that, in spite of the name of its author, a built St. Dié would, probably, have been the reverse of successful; that St. Dié illustrates, as clearly as possible, the dilemma of the free standing building, the space occupier attempting to act as space definer? For, if it is to be doubted whether this 'centre' would facilitate confluence, then, regardless of the desirability of this effect, it seems that what we are here provided with is a kind of unfulfilling schizophrenia—an acropolis of sorts which is attempting to perform as some version of an agora!

However, in spite of the anomaly of the undertaking, the re-affirmation of centralizing themes was not readily to be relinquished; and, if the 'core of the city' argument might easily be interpreted as a seepage of townscape strategies into the CIAM city diagram, a point may now be made by bringing the St. Dié city centre into comparison with that of the approximately contemporary Harlow new town which, though evidently 'impure,' may not be quite so implausible as, sometimes, has appeared to be the case.

At Harlow, where there is absolutely no by-play with metaphors of acropolis, there can be no doubt that what one is being offered is a 'real' and literal market-place; and, accordingly, the discrete aspects of the individual buildings are played down, the buildings themselves amalgamated, to appear as little more than a casually haphazard defining wrapper. But, if the Harlow town square, supposed to be the authentic thing itself, a product of the vicissitudes of time and all the rest, may be a little over-ingratiating in its illusory appeal, if one might be just a little fatigued with quite so enticing a combination of instant 'history' and overt 'modernity,' if its simulation of medieval space may still appear believable as one stands

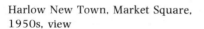

Harlow New Town, Market Square, 1950s, view

inside it, then, as curiosity becomes aroused, even this illusion quickly disappears.

For an overview or quick dash behind the immediately visible set piece rapidly discloses the information that what one has been subjected to is little more than a stage set. That is, the space of the square, professing to be an alleviation of density, the relief of an impacted context, quickly lends itself to be read as nothing of the kind. It exists without essential back up or support, without pressure, in built or human form, to give credibility or vitality to its existence; and, with the space thus fundamentally 'unexplained,' it becomes apparent that, far from being any outcropping of an historical or spatial context (which it would seem to be), the Harlow town square is, in effect, a foreign body interjected into a garden suburb without benefit of quotation marks.

But, in the issue of Harlow versus St. Dié, one is still obliged to recognize a coincidence of intention. In both cases the object is the production of a significant urban foyer; and, given this aim, it seems perfectly fair to say

Harlow New Town, Market Square, 1950s, air view

that, whatever its merits as architecture, the Harlow town square provides a closer approximation to the imagined condition than ever St. Dié might have done. Which is neither to endorse Harlow nor condemn St. Dié; but is rather to allow them both, as attempts to simulate the qualities of 'solid' city with the elements of 'void,' to emerge as comparable gestures of interrogation.

Now, as to the relevance of the questions which they propound, this might be best examined by once more directing attention to the typical format of the traditional city which, in every way, is so much the inverse of the city of modern architecture that the two of them together might, sometimes, almost present themselves as the alternative reading of some Gestalt diagram illustrating the fluctuations of the figure-ground phenomenon. Thus, the one is almost all white, the other almost all black; the one an accumulation of solids in largely unmanipulated void, the other an accumulation of voids in largely unmanipulated solid; and, in both cases, the fundamental ground promotes an entirely different category of figure—in the one *object*, in the other *space*.

However not to comment upon this somewhat ironical condition; and simply, in spite of its obvious defects, to notice very briefly the apparent virtues of the traditional city: the solid and continuous matrix or texture giving energy to its reciprocal condition, the specific space; the

Le Corbusier: project for Saint-Dié, figure-ground plan

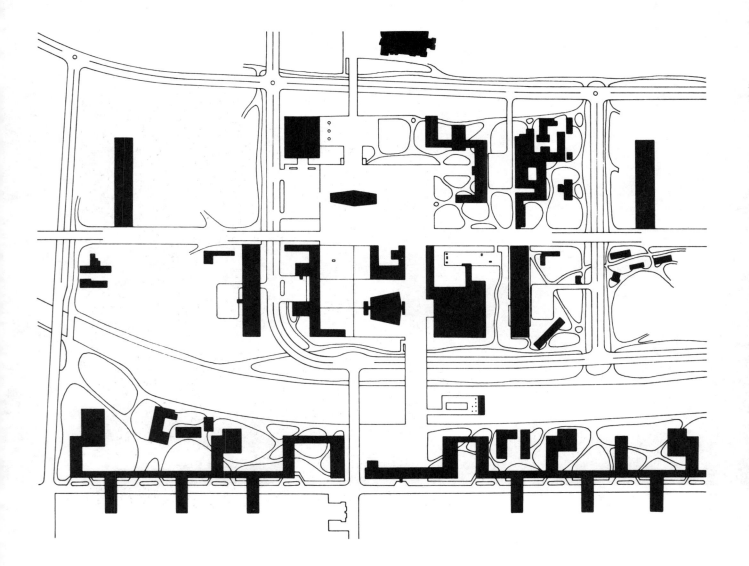

ensuing square and street acting as some kind of public relief valve and providing some condition of legible structure; and, just as important, the very great versatility of the supporting texture or ground. For, as a condition of virtually continuous building of incidental make up and assignment, this is not under any great pressure for self-completion or overt expression of function; and, given the stabilizing effects of public façade, it remains relatively free to act according to local impulse or the requirements of immediate necessity.

Perhaps these are virtues which scarcely require to be proclaimed; but, if they are, everyday, more loudly asserted, the situation so described is still not quite tolerable. If it offers a debate between solid and void, public stability and private unpredictability, public figure and private ground which has not failed to stimulate, and if the object building, the soap bubble of sincere internal expression, when taken as a universal proposition, represents nothing short of a demolition of public life and decorum, if it reduces the public realm, the traditional world of visible civics to an amorphic remainder, one is still largely impelled to say: so what? And it is the logical, defensible presuppositions of modern architecture—light, air, hygiene, aspect, prospect, recreation, movement, openness—which inspire this reply.

So, if the sparse, anticipatory city of isolated objects and continuous

Parma, figure-ground plan

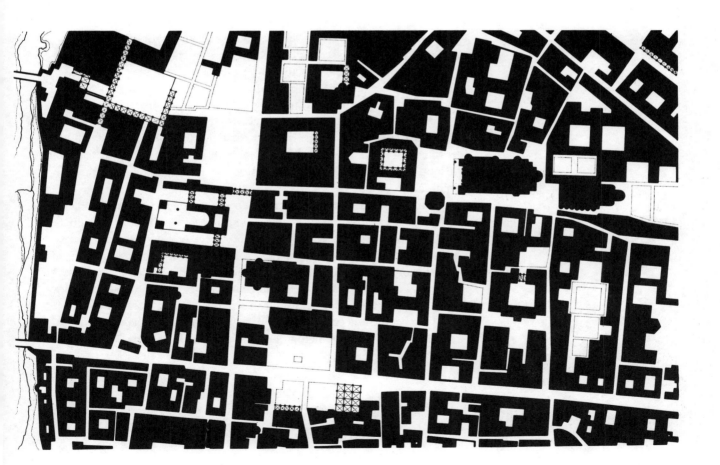

voids, the alleged city of freedom and 'universal' society will not be made
to go away and if, perhaps, in its essentials, it is more valuable than its dis-
creditors can allow, if, while it is felt to be 'good', nobody seems to like it,
the problem remains: what to try to do with it?

There are various possibilities. To adopt an ironical posture or to
propound social revolution are two of them; but, since the possibilities
of simple irony are almost totally pre-empted and since revolution tends
to turn into its opposite, then, in spite of the persistent devotees of absolute
freedom, it is to be doubted whether either of these are very useful
strategies. To propose that more of the same, or more of approximately
the same, will—like old-fashioned *laissez faire*—provide self-correction?
This is just as much to be doubted as is the myth of the unimpaired
capacities of self-regulating capitalism; but, all of these possibilities apart,
it would seem, first of all, to be reasonable and plausible to examine the
threatened or promised city of object fixation from the point of view of the
possibility of its perception.

It is a matter of how much the mind and eye can absorb or comprehend; and it is a problem which has been around, without any successful solution, since the later years of the eighteenth century. The issue is
that of quantification.

Pancras is like Marylebone, Marylebone is like Paddington; all the streets
resemble each other ... your Gloucester Places, and Baker Streets, and
Harley Streets, and Wimpole Streets ... all of those flat, dull, spiritless
streets, resembling each other like a large family of plain children, with
Portland Place and Portman Square for their respectable parents.[8]

The time is 1847 and the judgement, which is Disraeli's, may be taken as
a not so early reaction to the disorientations produced by repetition. But,
if the multiplication of spaces long ago began to elicit such disgust, then
what is there now to be said about the proliferation of objects? In other
words, whatever may be said about the traditional city, is it possible that
the city of modern architecture can sustain anything like so adequate a
perceptual base? And the obvious answer would seem to be not. For it is
surely apparent that, while limited structured spaces may facilitate
identification and understanding, an interminable naturalistic void
without any recognizable boundaries will at least be likely to defeat all
comprehension.

Certainly, in considering the modern city from the point of view of
perceptual performance, by *Gestalt* criteria it can only be condemned.
For, if the appreciation or perception of object or figure is assumed to
require the presence of some sort of ground or field, if the recognition of
some sort of however closed field is a prerequisite of all perceptual experience and, if consciousness of field precedes consciousness of figure, then,
when figure is unsupported by any recognizable frame of reference, it
can only become enfeebled and self-destructive. For, while it is possible to
imagine—and to imagine being delighted by—a field of objects which are

legible in terms of proximity, identity, common structure, density, etc., there are still questions as to how much such objects can be agglomerated and of how plausible, in reality, it is to assume the possibility of their exact multiplication. Or, alternatively, these are questions relative to optical mechanics, of how much can be supported before the trade breaks down and the introduction of closure, screening, segregation of information, becomes an experiential imperative.

Presumably this point has not, as yet, quite been reached. For the modern city in its cut-price versions (the city in the park become the city in the parking lot), for the most part still exists within the closed fields which the traditional city supplies. But, if, in this way—not only perceptually but also sociologically parasitic, it continues to feed off the organism which it proposes to supplant, then the time is now not very far remote when this sustaining background may finally disappear.

Such is the incipient crisis of more than perception. The traditional city goes away; but even the parody of the city of modern architecture refuses to become established. The public realm has shrunk to an apologetic ghost but the private realm has not been significantly enriched; there are no references—either historical or ideal; and, in this atomized society, except for what is electronically supplied or is reluctantly sought in print, communication has either collapsed or reduced itself to impoverished interchange of ever more banal verbal formulae.

Evidently, it is not necessary that the dictionary, whether Webster or OED, need retain its present volume. It is redundant; its bulk is inflated; the indiscriminate use of its contents lends itself to specious rhetoric; its sophistications have very little to do with the values of 'jus' plain folks'; and, certainly, its semantic categories very little correspondence with the intellectual processes of the neo-noble savage. But, if the appeal, in the name of innocence, seriously to abbreviate the dictionary *might* find only a minimum of support, even though built forms are not quite the same as words, we have here sketched a programme strictly analogous to that which was launched by modern architecture.

Let us eliminate the gratuitous; let us concern ourselves with needs rather than wants; let us not be too preoccupied with framing the distinctions; instead let us build from fundamentals...Something very like this was the message which led to the present impasse; and, if contemporary happenings are believed (like modern architecture itself) to be inevitable, of course, they will become so. But, on the other hand, if we do not suppose ourselves to be in the Hegelian grip of irreversible fate, it is just possible that there are alternatives to be found.

In any case the question at this point is not so much whether the traditional city, in absolute terms, is good or bad, relevant or irrelevant, in tune with the *Zeitgeist* or otherwise. Nor is it a question of modern architecture's obvious defects. Rather it is a question of common sense and common interest. We have two models of the city. Ultimately, wishing to surrender neither, we wish to qualify both. For in an age, allegedly, of

Vittoria, Spain, Plaza Mayor

Le Corbusier: Paris, Plan Voisin, 1925,
aerial axonometric

optional latitude and pluralist intention, it should be possible at least to plot some kind of strategy of accommodation and coexistence.

But, if in this way we now ask for deliverance from the city of deliverance, then in order to secure any approximation to this condition of freedom, there are certain cherished fantasies, not without final value, which the architect must be called upon to imagine as modified and re-directed. The notion of himself as messiah is one of these; and, while the notion of himself as eternal proponent of avant gardeism is another, even more important is the strangely desperate idea of architecture as oppressive and coercive.[9] Indeed, particularly, this curious relic of neo-Hegelianism will require to be temporarily suppressed; and this in the interests of a recognition that 'oppression' is always with us as the insuperable condition of existence—'oppression' of birth and death, of place and time, of language and education, of memory and numbers, being all of them components of a condition which, as yet, is not to be superseded.

And so to proceed from diagnosis—usually perfunctory—to prognosis—generally even more casual—firstly there might be suggested the overthrow of one of modern architecture's least avowed but most visible tenets. This is the proposition that all outdoor space must be in public ownership and accessible to everybody; and, if there is no doubt that this was a central working idea and, has, long since, become a bureaucratic cliché, there is still the obligation to notice that, among the repertory of possible ideas, the inordinate importance of this one is very odd indeed. And thus, while its iconographic substance may be recognized—it meant a collectivized and emancipated society which knew no artificial barriers— one may still marvel that such an offbeat proposition could ever have become so established. One walks through the city—whether it is New York, Rome, London or Paris who cares; one sees lights upstairs, a ceiling, shadows, some objects; but, as one mentally fills in the rest and imagines a society of unexampled brilliance from which one is fatally excluded, one does not feel exactly deprived. For, in this curious commerce between the visible and the undisclosed, we are well aware that we too can erect our own private proscenium and, by turning on our own lights, augment the general hallucination which, however absurd it may be, is never other than stimulating.

This is to specify, in a particularly extreme form, a way in which exclusion may gratify the imagination. One is called upon to complete apparently mysterious but really normal situations of which one is made only partially aware; and, if literally to penetrate all these situations would be destructive of speculative pleasure, one might now apply the analogy of the illuminated room to the fabric of the city as a whole. Which is quite simply to say that the absolute spatial freedoms of the *ville radieuse* and its more recent derivatives are without interest; and that, rather than being empowered to walk everywhere—everwhere being always the same—almost certainly it would be more satisfying to be presented with

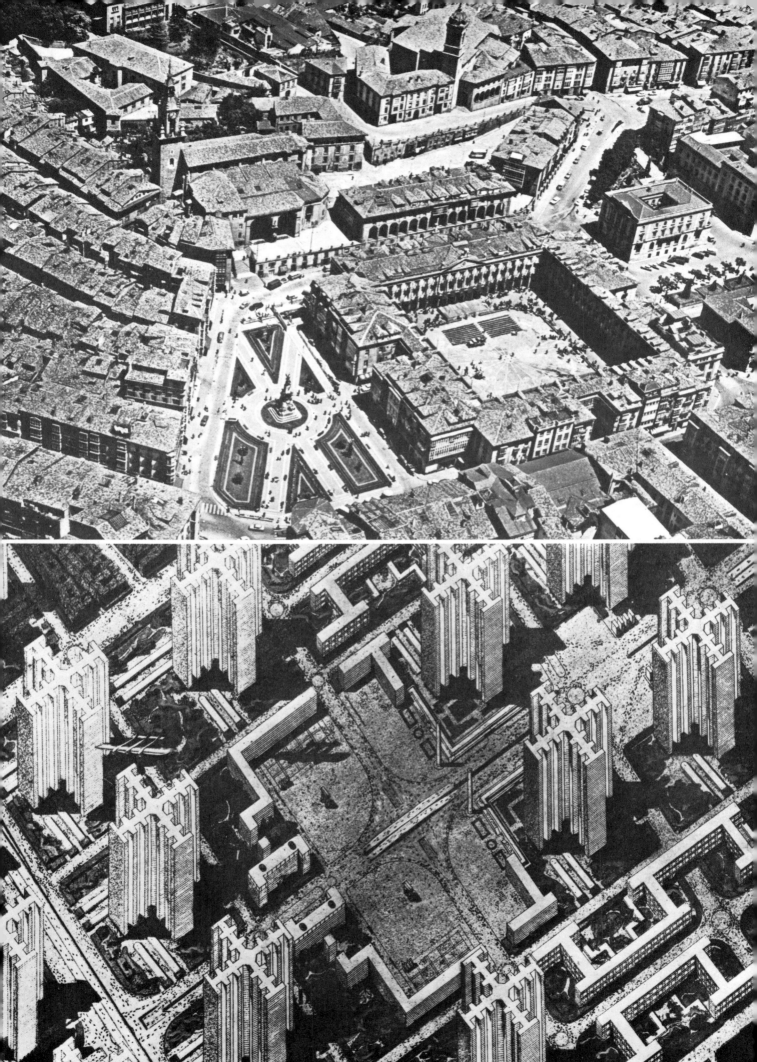

Uffizi, air view

the exclusions—wall, railings, fences, gates, barriers—of a reasonably constructed ground plane.

However, if to say so much is only to articulate what is already a dimly perceived tendency, and if it is usually provided with sociological justification[10] (identity, collective 'turf', etc.), there are more important sacrifices of contemporary tradition which are surely required; and we speak of a willingness to reconsider the object which allegedly nobody wants and to evaluate it not so much as figure but as ground.

A proposal which, for practical purposes, demands a willingness to imagine the present dispensation as inverted, the idea of such inversion is most immediately and succinctly to be explained by the comparison of a void and a solid of almost identical proportions. And, if to illustrate prime solid nothing will serve better than Le Corbusier's Unité, then, as an instance of the opposite and reciprocal condition, Vasari's Uffizi could scarcely be more adequate. The parallel is, of course, trans-cultural; but, if a sixteenth century office building become a museum may, with certain reservations, be brought into critical proximity with a twentieth century apartment house, then an obvious point can be made. For, if the Uffizi is Marseilles turned outside in, or if it is a jelly mould for the Unité, it is also void become figurative, active and positively charged; and, while the effect of Marseilles is to endorse a private and atomized society, the Uffizi is much more completely a 'collective' structure. And, to further bias the comparison: while Le Corbusier presents a private and insulated building which, unambiguously, caters to a limited clientèle, Vasari's model is sufficiently two-faced to be able to accommodate a good deal more. Urbanistically it is far more active. A central void-figure, stable and obviously planned, with, by way of entourage, an irregular back up which may be loose and responsive to close context. A stipulation of an ideal world and an engagement of empirical circumstance, the Uffizi may be seen as reconciling themes of self-conscious order and spontaneous randomness; and, while it accepts the existing, by then proclaiming the new the Uffizi confers value upon both new and old.

Again, a comparison of a Le Corbusier product, this time with one by Auguste Perret, may be used to expand or to reinforce the preceding; and, since the comparison, originally made by Peter Collins, involves two interpretations of the same programme, it may, to that extent, be considered the more legitimate. Le Corbusier and Perret's projects for the Palace of the Soviets which, the two together, might have been designed to confound the proposition that form follows function, could almost be allowed to speak for themselves. Perret gestures to immediate context and Le Corbusier scarcely so. With their explicit spatial connections with the Kremlin and the inflection of their courtyard towards the river, Perret's buildings enter into an idea of Moscow which they are evidently intended to elaborate; but Le Corbusier's buildings, which are apt to proclaim their derivation from internal necessity, are certainly not so much responsive to the site as they are symbolic constructs supposedly

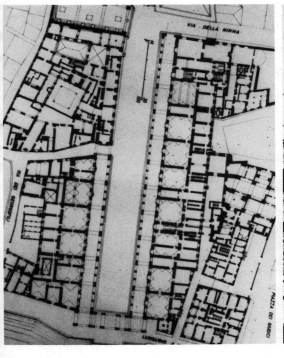

Florence, Uffizi, plan

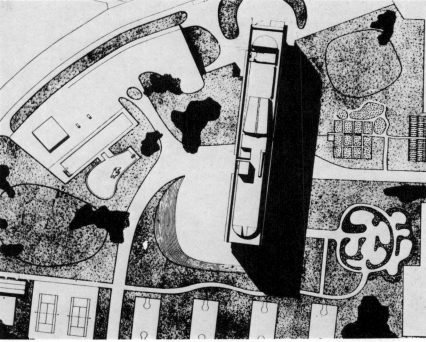

Le Corbusier: Marseilles, Unité
d'Habitation, 1946, site plan

Unité d'Habitation, view

Uffizi, view

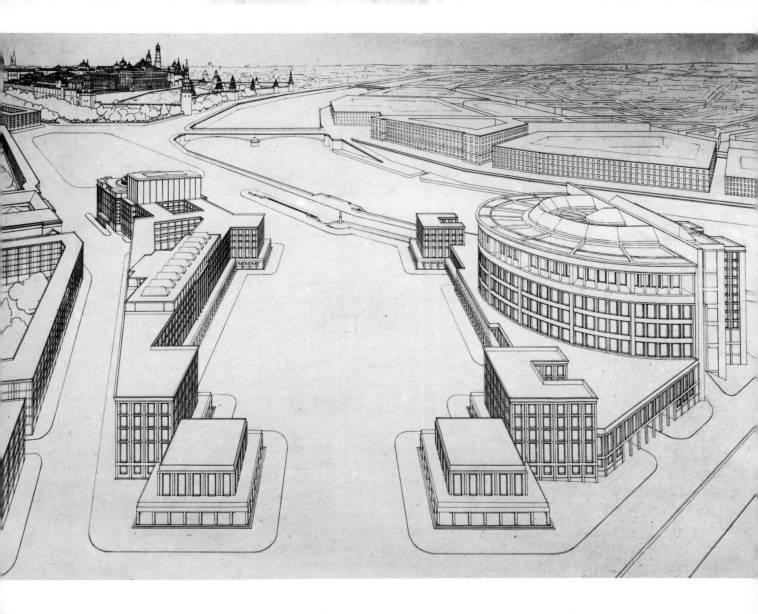

responsive to an assumed newly liberated cultural milieu. And if in each case, the use of site is iconographically representative of an attitude to tradition, then, in these two evaluations of tradition, it may be entirely fair to read the effects of a twenty year generation gap.

But in one further parallel along these lines there is no such gap that can be interposed. Gunnar Asplund and Le Corbusier were entirely of the same generation; and, if one is here not dealing with comparable programmes or proposals of equivalent size, the dates of Asplund's Royal Chancellery project (1922) and Le Corbusier's Plan Voisin (1925) may still facilitate their joint examination. The Plan Voisin is an outgrowth of Le Corbusier's Ville Contemporaine of 1922. It is the Ville Contemporaine injected into a specific Parisian site; and, however unvisionary it was professed to be—indeed however 'real' it has become—it evidently

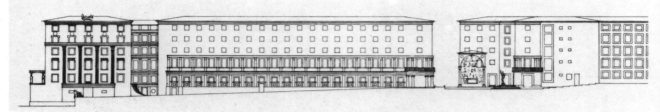

above
Le Corbusier: Paris, Plan Voisin, 1925, perspective

below
Gunnar Asplund: Stockholm, project for the Royal Chancellery, 1922, elevation

therefore quoting asplund is architecturally 'political' too

proposes a completely different working model of reality from that employed by Asplund. The one is a statement of historical destiny, the other of historical continuity; the one is a celebration of generalities, the other of specifics; and, in both cases, the site functions as icon representative of these different evaluations.

Thus, as almost always in his urbanistic proposals, Le Corbusier largely responds to the idea of a reconstructed society and is largely unconcerned with local spatial minutiae. If the Portes Saint-Denis and Saint-Martin may be incorporated in the city centre so far so good; if the Marais is to be destroyed no matter; the principal aim is manifesto. Le Corbusier is primarily involved with the building of a Phoenix symbol; and, in his concern to illustrate a new world rising above the ashes of the old, one may detect a reason for his highly perfunctory approach to major monuments—only to be inspected after cultural inoculation. And thus, by contrast, Asplund for whom, one might suppose, ideas of social continuity become represented in his attempt to make of his buildings, as much as possible, a part of the urban continuum.

But, if Le Corbusier simulates a future and Asplund a past, if one is almost all prophecy theatre and the other almost all memory, and if it is the present contention that both of these ways of looking at the city—spatially as well as sentimentally—are valuable, the immediate concern is with their spatial implications. We have identified two models; we have suggested that it would be less than sane to abandon either; and we are, consequently, concerned with their reconciliation, with, at one level, a recognition of the specific and, at another, the possibilities of general statement. But there is also the problem of one model which is active and predominant and another which is highly recessive; and it is in order to correct this lack of equilibrium that we have been obliged to introduce Vasari, Perret and Asplund as purveyors of useful information. And, if there is no doubt about it that, of the three, Perret is the most banal and, maybe, Vasari the most suggestive, then, probably, Asplund may be felt to illustrate the most elaborate use of multiple design strategies. Simultaneously the empiricist reacting to site and the idealist concerned with

right
Asplund: Chancellery, site plan

below
Asplund: Chancellery, plan

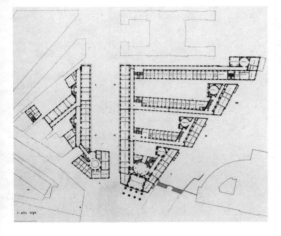

right
Le Corbusier: Paris, Plan Voisin,
site plan

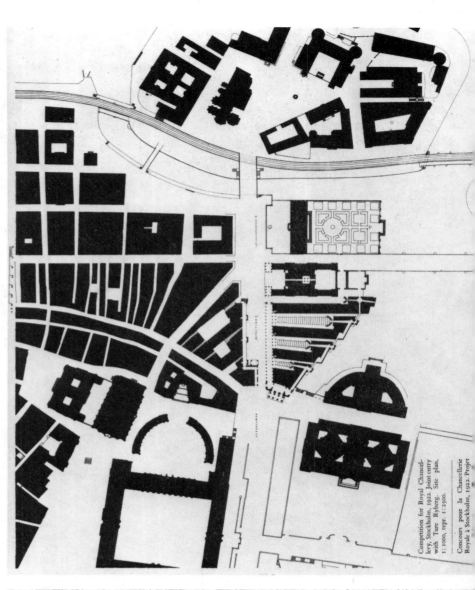

Competition for Royal Chancellery, Stockholm, 1922. Joint entry with Ture Ryberg. Site plan, 1:1000, repr. 1:2500.

Concours pour la Chancellerie Royale à Stockholm, 1922. Projet

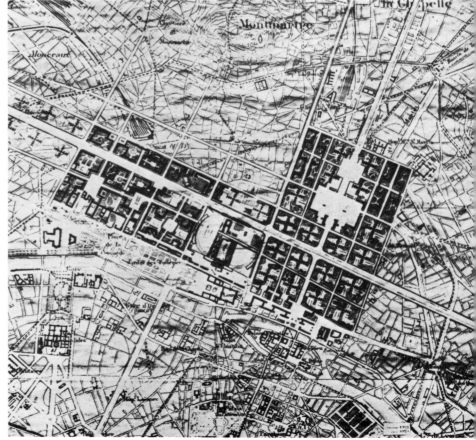

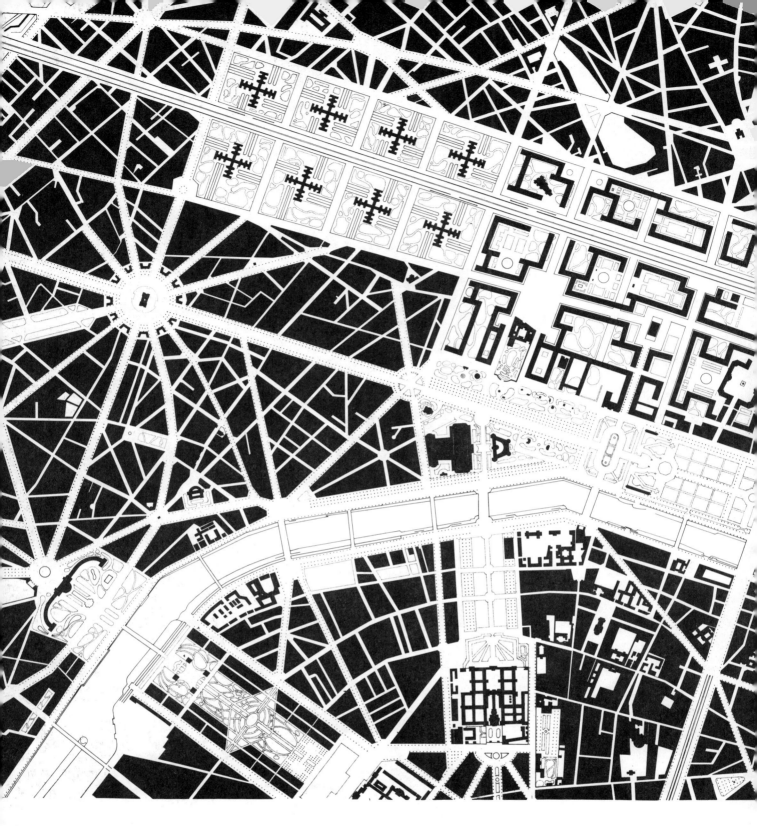

Le Corbusier: Paris, Plan Voisin, 1925,
figure-ground plan

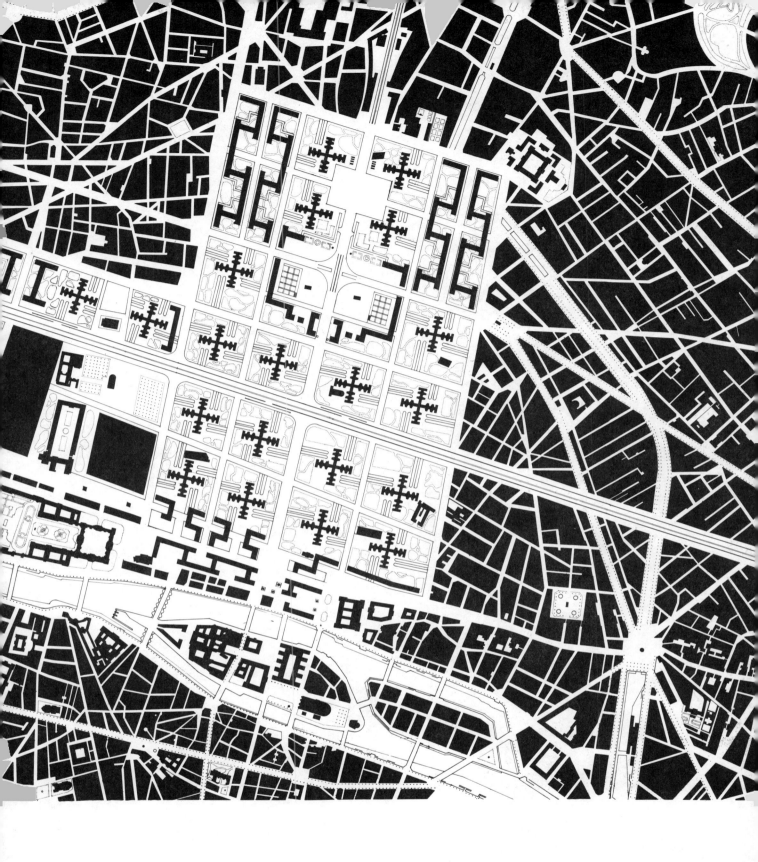

Vue générale de la Place et du Palais.

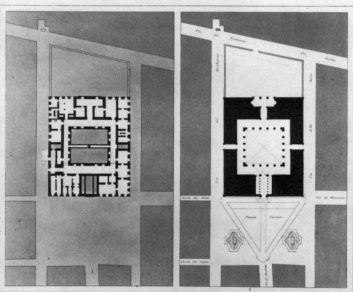

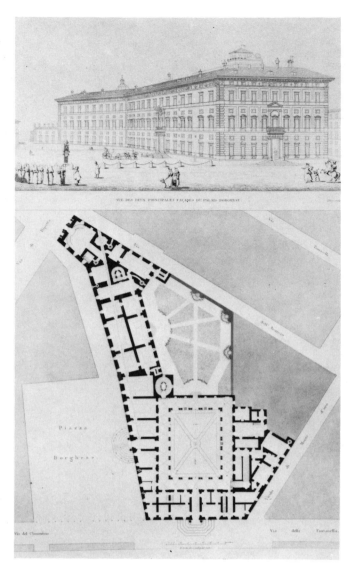

VUE DES DEUX PRINCIPALES FAÇADES DU PALAIS BORGHESE.

normative condition, in one work he responds, adjusts, translates, asserts to be—and all at once—passive recipient and active reverberator.

However, Asplund's play with assumed contingencies and assumed absolutes, brilliant though it may be, does seem to involve mostly strategies of response; and, in considering problems of the object, it may be useful to consider the admittedly ancient technique of deliberately distorting what is also presented as the ideal type. And to take a Renaissance-Baroque example: if Santa Maria della Consolazione at Todi may, in spite of certain provincial details, be allowed to represent the 'perfect' building in all its pristine integrity, then how is this building to be 'compromised' for use in a less than 'perfect' site? This is a problem which a functionalist theory could neither envisage nor admit. For though, in practice, functionalism could often become compounded with a theory of types, intrinsically it was scarcely able to comprehend the notion of already synthesized and pre-existent models being shifted around from place to place. But, if functionalism proposed an end to typologies in favour of a logical induction from concrete facts, it is precisely because it was unwilling to consider iconic significance as a concrete fact in itself, unwilling to imagine particular physical configurations as instruments of communication, that functionalism can have very little to say with reference to the deformation of ideal models. So Todi we know to be a sign and an advertisement; and, as we concede the freedom to use the advertisement wherever conditions may require it, we also infer the possibilities of sustaining, or salvaging the meaning while manipulating the form according to the exigencies of circumstance. And, in such terms, it may be possible to see Sant' Agnese in Piazza Navona as a Todi which is simultaneously 'compromised' and intact. The constricted site propounds its pressures; the piazza and the dome are the irreducible protagonists in a debate; the piazza has something to say about Rome, the dome about cosmic fantasy; and, finally, via a process of response and challenge, both of them make their point.

So the reading of Sant' Agnese continuously fluctuates between an interpretation of the building as object and its reinterpretation as texture; but, if the church may be sometimes an ideal object and sometimes a function of the piazza wall, yet another Roman instance of such figure—ground alternation—of both meanings and forms—might still be cited. Obviously not so elaborate a construct as Sant' Agnese, the Palazzo Borghese, located upon its highly idiosyncratic site, contrives both to respond to this site and to behave as a representative palace of the Farnese type. The Palazzo Farnese provides its reference and meaning. It contributes certain factors of central stability, both of façade and plan; but, with the 'perfect' *cortile* now embedded in a volume of highly 'imperfect' and elastic perimeter, with the building predicated on a recognition of both archetype and accident, there follows from this duplicity of evaluation an internal situation of great richness and freedom.

Now this type of strategy which combines local concessions with

far left above
Rome, Palazzo Farnese, view and plan

left above
Rome, Palazzo Borghese, view and plan

far left below
Todi, Santa Maria della Consolazione

left below
Rome, Sant' Agnese in Piazza Navona

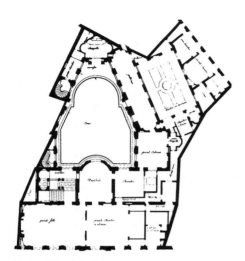

Paris, Hotel de Beauvais, plan

Hotel de Beauvais, elevation

Le Corbusier: Villa Savoye at Poissy

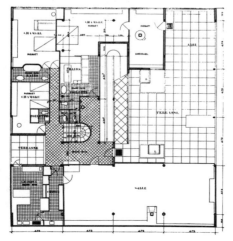

Villa Savoye, plan

a declaration of independence from anything local and specific could be indefinitely illustrated; but, perhaps, one more instance of it will suffice. Le Pautre's Hôtel de Beauvais, with its ground floor of shops, is externally something of a minor Roman *palazzo* brought to Paris; and, as an even more elaborate version of a category of free plan, it might possibly prompt comparison with the great master and advocate of the free plan himself. But Le Corbusier's technique is, of course, the logical opposite to that of Le Pautre; and, if the 'freedoms' of the Villa Savoye depend on the stability of its indestructible perimeter, the 'freedoms' of the Hôtel de Beauvais are derived from the equivalent stability of its central *cour d'honneur*.

In other words, one might almost write an equation: Uffizi: Unité= Hôtel de Beauvais: Villa Savoye; and, as a simple convenience, this equation is of completely crucial importance. For on the one hand at the Villa Savoye, as at the Unité, there is an absolute insistence upon the virtues of primary solid, upon the isolation of the building as object and the urbanistic corollary of this insistence scarcely requires further commentary; and, on the other, in the Hôtel de Beauvais, as at the Palazzo Borghese, the built solid is allowed to assume comparatively minor significance. Indeed, in these last cases, the built solid scarcely divulges itself; and, while unbuilt space (courtyard) assumes the directive role, becomes the predominant idea, the building's perimeter is enabled to act as no more than a 'free' response to adjacency. On the one side of the equation building becomes prime and insulated, on the other the isolation of identifiable space reduces (or elevates) the status of building to infill.

But building as infill! The idea *can* seem to be deplorably passive and empirical–though such need not be the case. For, in spite of their spatial preoccupations neither the Hôtel de Beauvais or the Palazzo Borghese are, finally, flaccid. They, both of them, assert themselves by way of representational façade, by way of progression from façade-figure (solid) to courtyard-figure (void); and, in this context, although the Villa Savoye is by no means the simplistic construct which we have here made it appear (although it too, to some extent, operates as its opposite) for present purposes its arguments are not central.

For, far more clearly than at Savoye, at the Hôtel de Beauvais and the Palazzo Borghese the *Gestalt* condition of ambivalence–double value and double meaning–results in interest and provocation. However, though speculation may thus be incited by the fluctuations of the figure-ground phenomenon (which may be volatile or may be sluggish), the possibilities of any such activity–especially at an urban scale–would seem very largely to depend upon the presence of what used to be called *poché*.

Frankly, we had forgotten the term, or relegated it to a catalogue of obsolete categories; and were only recently reminded of its usefulness by Robert Venturi.[11] But if *poché*, understood as the imprint upon the plan of the traditional heavy structure, acts to disengage the principal spaces of the building from each other, if it is a solid matrix which frames a series of major spatial events, it is not hard to acknowledge that the recognition of *poché* is also a matter of context and that, depending on perceptual field, a building itself may become a type of *poché*, for certain purposes a solid assisting the legibility of adjacent spaces. And thus, for instance, such buildings as the Palazzo Borghese may be taken as types of habitable *poché* which articulate the transition of external voids.

So, thus far, implicitly, we have been concerned with an appeal for urban *poché* and the argument has been primarily buttressed by perceptual criteria; but, if the same argument might, just as well, receive sociological support (and we would prefer to see the two findings as interrelated), we must still face a very brief question of how to do it.

It seems that the general usefulness of *poché* in a revived and over-hauled sense, comes by its ability, as a solid, to engage or be engaged by adjacent voids, to act as both figure and ground as necessity or circum-stance might require; but with the city of modern architecture, of course, no such reciprocity is either possible or intended. But, though the employment of ambiguous resources might foul the cleanliness of this city's mission, since we are involved in this process anyway, it will be opportune again to produce the Unité and, this time, to bring it into confrontation with the Quirinale. In plan configuration, in its nimble relationship with the ground and in the equality of its two major faces the Unité ensures its own emphatic isolation. A housing block which, more or less, satisfies desired requirements in terms of exposure, ventilation, etc., its limitations with regard to collectivity and context have already been noted; and it is in order to examine possible alleviation of these shortcomings that the Palazzo del Quirinale is now introduced. In its extension, the improbably attenuated Manica Lunga (which might be several Unités put end to end), the Quirinale carries within its general format all the possibilities of positive twentieth century living standards (access, light, air, aspect, prospect, etc.); but, while the Unité continues to enforce its isolation and object quality, the Quirinale extension acts in quite a different way.

Thus, with respect to the street on the one side and its gardens on the other, the Manica Lunga acts as both space *occupier* and space *definer*, as positive figure and passive ground, permitting both street and garden to exert their distinct and independent personalities. To the street it projects a hard, 'outside' presence which acts as a kind of datum to service a con-dition of irregularity and circumstance (Sant' Andrea, etc.) across the way; but, while in this manner it establishes the public realm, it is also able to secure for the garden side a wholly contrary, softer, private and, potent-ially, more adaptable condition.

The elegance and the economy of the operation, all done with so little and all so obvious, may stand as a criticism of contemporary pro-cedures; but, if a consideration of perhaps more than one building has here been implied, such an expansion may be carried a little further. To consider, for instance, the courtyard of the Palais Royal, admired but not 'used' by Le Corbusier, as providing a clear differentiation between an internal condition of relative privacy and an external, less comprehensible

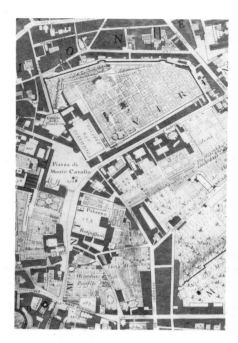

above
Rome, the Quirinale and its vicinity,
1748, from the plan of Nolli

right
Rome, the Quirinale, air view

below right
Rome, the Quirinale and Manica Lunga

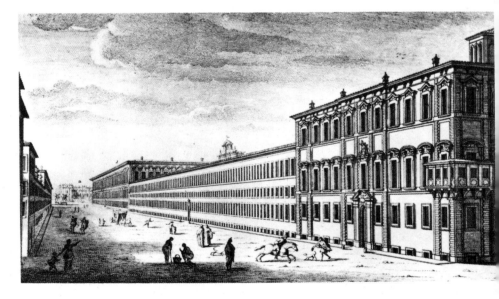

Paris, courtyard of the Palais Royal

Paris, the Louvre, Tuileries, and Palais Royal, c.1780, figure-ground plan

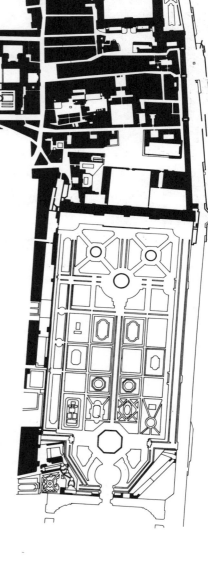

Paris, the Louvre, Tuileries, and Palais Royal, from the Plan Turgot, 1739

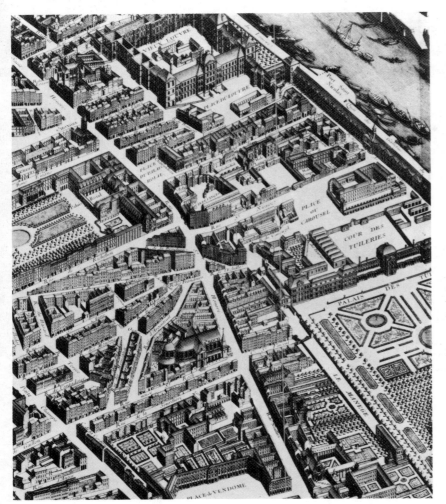

Wiesbaden, c.1900, figure-ground plan

world; to consider it not only as habitable *poché* but as an urban room, perhaps one of many; and to consider then a number of towers, current specification—smooth, bumpy, with or without entrails, whatever—to be located as urban furniture, perhaps some inside the 'room' and some outside. The order of the furniture is no matter; but the Palais Royal thus becomes an instrument of field recognition, an identifiable stabilizer and a means of collective orientation. The combination provides a condition of mutual reference, complete reciprocity, relative freedom. In addition, being essentially foolproof, it might almost 'make the evil difficult and the good easy.'[12]

That all this is of no consequence...? That between architecture and human 'activity' there is no relationship...? Such one knows to be the continuing prejudice of the 'Let us evaporate the object, let us interact' school; but, if existing political structure–whatever one might wish–seems scarcely to be upon the threshold of impending dissolution and if the object seems equally intractable to important physico-chemical decomposition, then, by way of reply, it *might* be arguable that it *could* be justifiable to make at least *some* concessions to these circumstances.

To summarize: it is here proposed that, rather than hoping and waiting for the withering away of the object (while, simultaneously manufacturing versions of it in profusion unparalleled), it might be judicious, in most cases, to allow and encourage the object to become digested in a prevalent texture or matrix. It is further suggested that neither object nor space fixation are, in themselves, any longer representative of valuable attitudes. The one may, indeed, characterize the 'new' city and the other the old; but, if these are situations which must be transcended rather than emulated, the situation to be hoped for should be recognized as one in which both buildings *and* spaces exist in an equality of sustained debate. A debate in which victory consists in each component emerging undefeated, the imagined condition is a type of solid-void dialectic which might allow for the joint existence of the overtly planned and the genuinely unplanned, of the set-piece and the accident, of the public and the private, of the state and the individual. It is a condition of alerted equilibrium which is envisaged; and it is in order to illuminate the potential of such a contest that we have introduced a rudimentary variety of possible strategies. Cross-breeding, assimilation, distortion, challenge, response, imposition, superimposition, conciliation: these might be given any number of names and, surely, neither can nor should be too closely specified; but if the burden of the present discussion has rested upon the city's morphology, upon the physical and inanimate, neither 'people' nor 'politics' are assumed to have been excluded. Indeed, both 'politics' and 'people' are, by now, clamouring for attention; but, if their scrutiny can barely be deferred, yet one more morphological stipulation may still be in order.

Ultimately, and in terms of figure-ground, the debate which is here postulated between solid and void is a debate between two models and, succinctly, these may be typified as acropolis and forum.

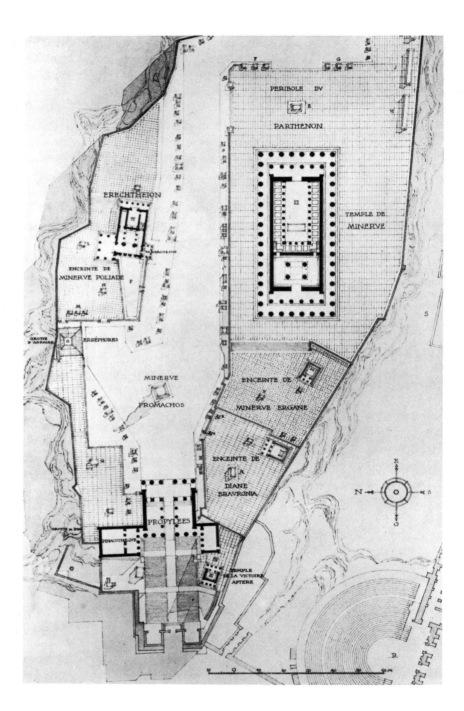

Athens, the acropolis

Rome, the imperial fora

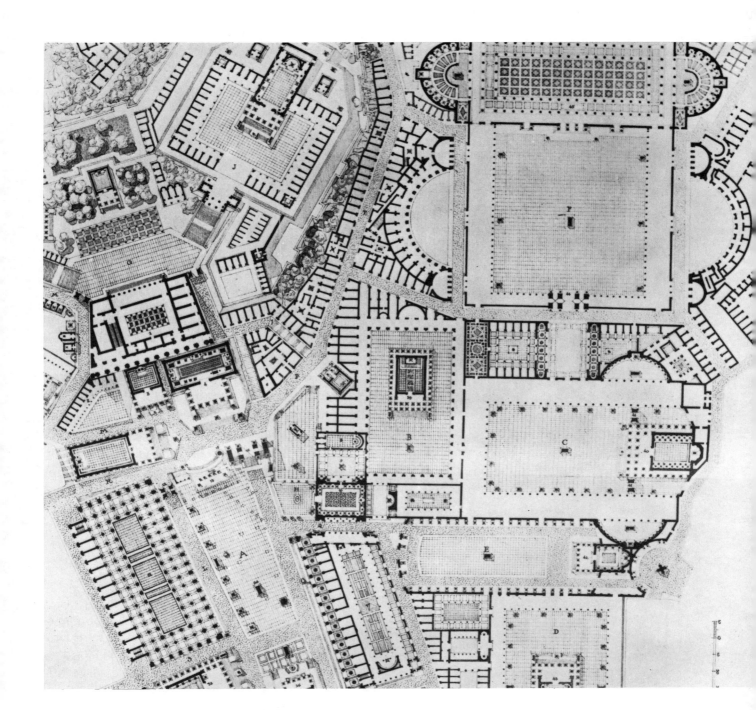

Collision City
and the Politics of 'Bricolage'

... if I have succeeded ... my last wish is that a higher and indestructible bond of the beautiful and the true may have been tied which will keep us forever firmly united. GEORG WILHELM FRIEDRICH HEGEL

... there exists a great chasm between those, on one side, who relate everything to a single central vision, one system less or more coherent or articulate, in terms of which they understand, think and feel–a single, universal, organizing principle in terms of which all that they are and say has significance–and, on the other side, those who pursue many ends, often unrelated and even contradictory, connected, if at all, only in some *de facto* way, for some psychological or physiological cause, related by no moral or aesthetic principle; these last lead lives, perform acts, and entertain ideas that are centrifugal rather than centripetal, their thought is scattered or diffused, moving on many levels, seizing upon the essence of a vast variety of experiences and objects, for what they are in themselves, without consciously or unconsciously seeking to fit them into or exclude them from any one unchanging ... at times fanatical, unitary inner vision. ISAIAH BERLIN

Scope of Total Architecture: such was the title which Walter Gropius affixed to a highly miscellaneous collection of, mostly, insubstantial essays. It was published in 1955; and, apparently, at that date, insistence on 'total architecture'–an obvious version of the Wagnerian *Gesamtkunstwerk* with all its promises of cultural integration–did not appear either unjustified or bizarre. Presumably, in 1955, a 'total architecture', an all controlling system which is yet not a system because it is a growth– 'a new growth coming right from the roots up'[1]–a combination, probably, of both Hegelian freedom and Hegelian necessity, in any case an emanation from fundamentals, was still considered not merely a plausible but also a desirable possibility; and, no doubt, it is here, when such notions become expressed in the gentle voice of 'concerned' liberalism, that we may be encouraged to discern something of the still shining afterglow of a unitary and holistic utopian faith.

We have earlier attempted to specify two versions of the utopian idea: utopia as an, implicit, object of contemplation and utopia as an, explicit, instrument of social change; and it is, at this stage, that we must re-affirm how much the conceptions of 'total architecture' and 'total design' are present, of necessity, in all utopian projections. Utopia has never offered options. The citizens of Thomas More's Utopia 'could not fail to be happy because they could not choose but be good'[2] and the idea of dwelling in 'goodness', without capacity for moral choice, has been prone to attend most fantasies, whether metaphorical or literal, of the ideal society.

For the architect, of course, the ethical content of the good society has, maybe, always been something which building was to make evident. Indeed it has, probably, always been his primary reference; for, whatever other controlling fantasies have emerged—antiquity, tradition, technology—these have invariably been conceived of as aiding and abetting an in some way benign or decorous social order.

Thus, not to retreat backwards all the way to Plato and, instead, to find a much more recent *quattrocento* springboard, Filarete's Sforzinda

Imperial Rome, model at the Museo della Civiltà Romana

contains all the premonitions of a situation assumed to be entirely susceptible to rule. There is a hierarchy of religious edifices, the princely *regia*, the aristocratic palace, the mercantile establishment, the private residence; and it is in terms of such a gradation—an ordering of status and function—that the well-conducted city became conceivable.

But it still remained an idea and there was to be no question of its literal and immediate application. For the medieval city represented an intractable nucleus of habit and interest which could, in no way, be directly breached; and, accordingly, the problem of the new became one of subversive interjection (Palazzo Massimo, Campidoglio, etc.) or of polemical demonstrations outside the city—the garden which discloses what the city ought to be.

The garden as criticism of the city—a criticism which the city later abundantly acknowledged—has not, as yet, received sufficient attention; but if, outside Florence, for instance, this theme is profusely represented, its most extreme affirmation can only be at Versailles, that seventeenth century criticism of medieval Paris which Haussmann and Napoleon III later so elaborately took to heart.

Clearly the gardens of Versailles, an aristocratic Disney World though they may have been, must, in the end, be construed as a Baroque attempt to put over *quattrocento* ideas; and it is when presented with this

Versailles, air view

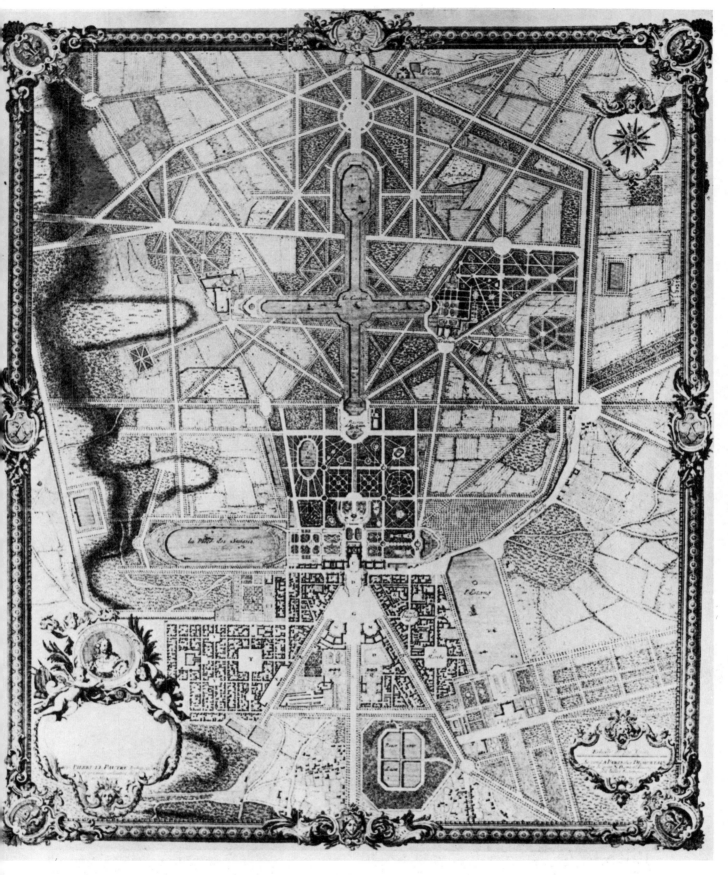

Versailles, plan

scene—still, occasionally, magnificent—that we are obliged to recognize how completely the lineaments of a Filarete style utopia could be replicated with trees. But, if Versailles might be interpreted as a utopia of reaction, we may still be amazed that the platonic, metaphorical utopia—generally regarded in Italy as such—could here be taken to such literal extremes.

Now, for present purposes, the obvious construct to mount alongside Versailles is the Villa Adriana at Tivoli. For, if the one is certainly an exhibition of total architecture and total design, the other attempts to dissimulate all reference to any controlling idea; and, if here there is absolute power under two impersonations, then one might even feel constrained to digress and to ask which is the more useful model—for us.

There is unambiguous, unabashed Versailles. The moral is declared to the world and the advertisement, like so many things French, can scarcely be refused. This is total control and the glaring illumination of it. It is the triumph of generality, the prevalence of the overwhelming idea and the refusal of the exception. And then, compared with this single-minded performance of Louis XIV, we have the curiosity of Hadrian—of Hadrian who is, apparently, so disorganized and casual, who proposes the reverse of any 'totality', who seems to need only an accumulation of disparate ideal fragments and whose criticism of Imperial Rome (configurationally much like his own house) is rather an endorsement than any protest.

But, if Versailles is the complete unitary model and the Villa Adriana

Tivoli, Hadrian's villa, view of model

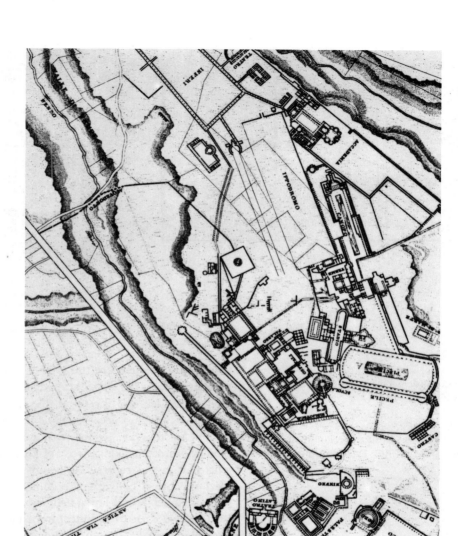

Hadrian's villa, plan after Luigi Canina

the apparently uncoordinated amalgam of discrete enthusiasms and, if the shattering ideality of Versailles is to be compared with the relativistically produced 'bits' of Tivoli, then what opportune interpretations can be placed upon this comparison? The obvious ones no doubt: that Versailles is the ultimate paradigm of autocracy; that it assumes a complete political power, undeviating in its objectives and long sustained; that, fundamentally, Hadrian was no less autocratic than Louis XIV but that, perhaps, he was not under the same compulsion to make so consistent a display of his autocracy.... But, if there is no doubt that all this might be said and if it is, after all, not very illuminating, it is at this stage that we feel obliged to call to our assistance Isaiah Berlin.

'The fox knows many things but the hedgehog knows one big thing.' This, in the area of our concern, is the statement, otherwise uninteresting, which, in *The Hedgehog and the Fox*, Isaiah Berlin chose to gloss and to elaborate.[3] Taken figuratively but not pressed too far, what one is sup-

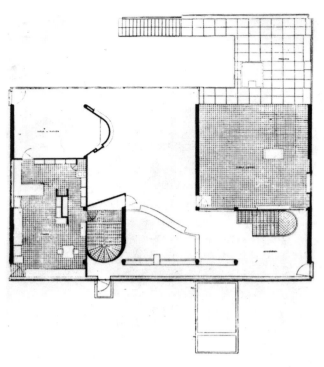

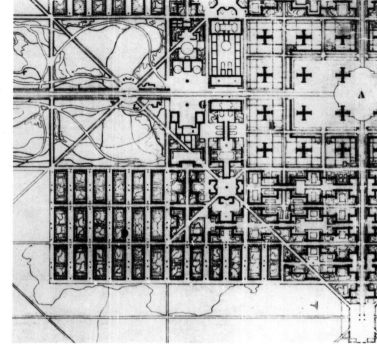

left
Le Corbusier: Villa Stein at Garches,
1927, plan

right
Le Corbusier: city for three million
inhabitants, 1922. Quadrant of plan

posed to have here are the types of two psychological orientations and temperaments, the one, the hedgehog, concerned with the primacy of the single idea and the other, the fox, preoccupied with multiplicity of stimulus; and the great ones of the earth divide fairly equally: Plato, Dante, Dostoevsky, Proust, are, needless to say, hedgehogs; Aristotle, Shakespeare, Pushkin, Joyce are foxes. This is the rough discrimination; but, if it is the representatives of literature and philosophy who are Berlin's critical concern, the game may be played in other areas also. Picasso, a fox, Mondrian, a hedgehog, the figures begin to leap into place; and, as we turn to architecture, the answers are almost entirely predictable. Palladio is a hedgehog, Giulio Romano a fox; Hawksmoor, Soane, Philip Webb are probably hedgehogs, Wren, Nash, Norman Shaw almost certainly foxes; and, closer to the present day, while Wright is unequivocally a hedgehog, Lutyens is just as obviously a fox.

But, to elaborate the results of, temporarily, thinking in such categories, it is as we approach the area of modern architecture that we begin to recognize the impossibility of arriving at any so symmetrical a balance. For, if Gropius, Mies, Hannes Meyer, Buckminster Fuller are clearly eminent hedgehogs, then where are the foxes whom we can enter into the same league? The preference is obviously one way. The 'single central vision' prevails. One notices a predominance of hedgehogs; but, if one might sometimes feel that fox propensities are less than moral and, therefore, not to be disclosed, of course there still remains the job of assigning to Le Corbusier his own particular slot, 'whether he is a monist or a pluralist, whether his vision is of one or of many, whether he is of a single substance or compounded of heterogeneous elements'.[4]

These are the questions which Berlin asks with reference to Tolstoy—questions which (he says) may not be wholly relevant; and then, very tentatively, he produces his hypothesis:

that Tolstoy was by nature a fox, but believed in being a hedgehog; that his gifts and achievements are one thing, and his beliefs, and consequently his interpretation of his own achievement, another; and that consequently his ideals have led him, and those whom his genius for persuasion has taken in, into a systematic misinterpretation of what he and others were doing or should be doing.[5]

Like so much other literary criticism shifted into a context of architectural focus, the formula seems to fit; and, if it should not be pushed too far, it can still offer partial explanation. There is Le Corbusier the architect with what William Jordy has called 'his witty and collisive intelligence'.[6] This is the person who sets up elaborately pretended platonic structures only to riddle them with an equally elaborate pretence of empirical detail, the Le Corbusier of multiple asides, cerebral references and complicated *scherzi*; and then there is Le Corbusier the urbanist, the deadpan protagonist of completely different strategies who, on a large and public scale, has the minimum of use for all the dialectical tricks and spatial involutions which, invariably, he considered the appropriate adornment of a more private situation. The public world is simple, the private world is elaborate; and, if the private world affects a concern for contingency, the would be public personality long maintained an almost too heroic disdain for any taint of the specific.

But, if the situation of *complex house–simple city* seems strange (when one might have thought that the reverse was applicable) and if to explain the discrepancy between Le Corbusier's architecture and his urbanism one might propose that he was, yet again, another case of a fox assuming hedgehog disguise for the purposes of public appearance, this is to build a digression into a digression. So we have noticed a relative absence of foxes at the present day; and, though this second digression may later, it is hoped, be put to use, the whole fox-hedgehog diversion was initiated for ostensibly other purposes—to establish Hadrian and Louis XIV as, more or less, free acting representatives of these two psychological types who were autocratically equipped to indulge their inherent propensities; and then to ask which of their two products might be felt to offer the more useful example for today—the accumulation of set-pieces in collision or the total co-ordinated display.

Which is in no way to doubt the pathological aspects of both Tivoli and Versailles but which is simply to assert their usefulness as exaggerations of any everyday norm. For, if these are laboratory specimens—surely no more, it is as two instances of the normal written very large that they might still address themselves to us to propound two questions: the one of taste, the other of politics.

Taste is, of course, no longer—and was, perhaps, never—a serious or substantial matter; but, this being said, it is almost certain that the uninhibited aesthetic preference of the present (given two conditions of almost equal size and endlessness) is for the structural discontinuities and the multiplicity of syncopated excitements which Tivoli presents. And, in the same way, whatever may be the contemporary and conscientious concern for 'the single central vision', it should be apparent that the manifold disjunctions of Hadrian's villa, the sustained inference that it was built by several people at different times, its seeming combination of the schizoid and the inevitable, might recommend it to the attention of political societies in which political power frequently—and mercifully—changes hands. For Hadrian's villa, as the simulated product of different régimes, all 'adds up'; and it adds up in so convincing and useful a fashion than one can only believe in its promotion.

However, this is to anticipate the argument, Hadrian here became inserted as a qualification and as a criticism of Louis XIV; and our initial surprise only concerned the fact that, at Versailles, even in the days of the platonic, metaphorical utopia, a genuinely determined hedgehog could come up with so literal a representation. Indeed one can only admire the will. Louis XIV was working against heavy odds; and, as soon as the classical utopia became superseded, there was patently involved a great liberation for people of his own particular personality type. Hadrian, with his reminiscences of famous buildings and places, provided, in his miniature 'Rome', a nostalgic and ecumenical illustration of the hybrid mix which the Empire presented. He was one of Françoise Choay's 'culturalists'; but, for Louis XIV, the 'progressivist' (assisted by Colbert), it is the rationalizable present and the future which exhibit themselves as the exacting idea; and, it is when the rationalizations of Colbert become handed down via Turgot to Saint-Simon and Comte that one begins to see something of Versailles's prophetic enormity.

For certainly, there was here anticipated all the myth of the rationally ordered and 'scientific' society; and, if we might find here—in more ways than one—a cause of the revolution of 1789, then we have only to imagine a later, post-revolutionary version of Louis XIV becoming supremely responsive to the message of Hegel. For in the history of despotism, as in the history of utopia, almost the same arguments seem to apply; and, as we are defeated in the area of the mechanically rational, so we move to the logic of organism.

But the combination of a mechanical model of rationality with an organic one could only be left to the later nineteenth century and to modern architecture; and it is, again, when we find these two hedgehog requirements conflated with the threat of damnation that we return to the activist utopian myth as it was received between the two world wars. The litany of the myth is by now familiar: a condition of violent and rapid change, unprecedented in the history of mankind, has produced a state of disorientation, of suffering, of exploitation so profound, a moral and political crisis of such dimension that catastrophe is surely imminent, perhaps inevitable; and, therefore, in order to ensure the orderly progression of human affairs, in order to guarantee universal mental and physical health, in order to avert the economic spoliations of working society, in order to avoid impending doom, the enterprises of mankind must be brought into a closer alignment with the, equally inevitable, forces of blissful destiny.

Such was the cult of crisis in the inter-war period. Before it is too late society must rid itself of outmoded sentiment, thought, technique; and,

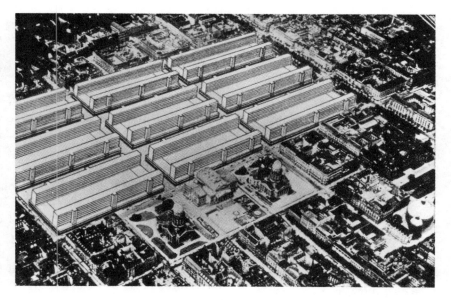

left
Tivoli, Hadrian's villa

right
Hilberseimer: project for Central
Berlin, 1927

if in order to prepare for its impending deliverance, it must be ready to
make *tabula rasa*, the architect, as key figure in this transformation, must
be prepared to assume the historical lead. For the built world of human
habitation and venture is the very cradle of the new order and, in order
properly to rock it, the architect must be willing to come forward, purged
of prejudice, as a front-line combatant in the battle for humanity.

Perhaps, while claiming to be scientific, the architect had never
previously operated within quite so fantastic a psycho-'political' milieu;
but, if this is to parenthesize, it was for such reasons—Pascalian reasons
of the heart—that the city became hypothesized as a condition of complete holistic and novel continuity, the result of scientific findings and a
completely glad, 'human', collaboration. Such became the activist
utopian total design. Perhaps an impossible vision (the future to approximate to the condition of Wagnerian music?) and certainly an improbable
thought; but the alternative, the disappearance of humanity, was
obviously far worse. And it is against such a psycho-cultural backdrop
that the message of modern architecture was marketed and sold.

For those who, during the past fifty or sixty years (and many of them
must be dead), have been anxiously awaiting the establishment of this
new city, it must have become increasingly clear that the promise—such
as it is—cannot be kept. Or so one might have thought; but, although
the total design message has had a somewhat spotted career and has often
elicited scepticism, it has remained, and possibly to this day, as the
psychological substratum of urban theory and its practical application.
Such a combination of scientism and moral enthusiasm was, of course,
long ago criticized by Karl Popper—perhaps most potently in his *Logic* of
Scientific Discovery and his *Poverty of Historicism*;[7] and in our own
interpretation of the activist utopia our indebtedness to Popper's position
should be evident. But if Popper, way back, was concerned with what
he maybe felt to be a situation of potentially dangerous rhetoric, in spite

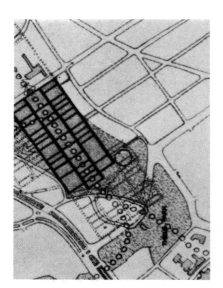

Candilis, Josic and Woods: Free
University of Berlin, 1964, plan

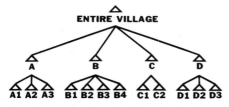

A1 contains requirements 7, 53, 57, 59, 60, 72, 125, 126, 128.
A2 contains requirements 31, 34, 36, 52, 54, 80, 94, 106, 136.
A3 contains requirements 37, 38, 50, 55, 77, 91, 103.
B1 contains requirements 39, 40, 41, 44, 51, 118, 127, 131, 138.
B2 contains requirements 30, 35, 46, 47, 61, 97, 98.

Christopher Alexander: diagram of a
village, 1964

of his easily available reservations, the total design message was not to
be repressed. Indeed it was so little to be repressed that, in the last few
years, a newly inspired and wholly literal version of the message was
enabled to appear as renditions of the 'systems' approach and a variety of
other methodological finds.

Now in these areas, where the 'science' of early modern architecture
is presumed to be painfully deficient, it goes without saying that the
methods involved are laborious and often extended. One has only to
contemplate the scrupulousness of the operation in a text such as *Notes
on the Synthesis of Form*[8] to get the picture. Obviously a 'clean' process
dealing with 'clean' information, atomized, cleaned and then cleaned
again, everything is ostensibly wholesome and hygienic; but, resulting
from the inhibiting characteristics of commitment, especially physical
commitment, the product seems never to be quite so prominent as the
process. And something comparable might be said about the related
production of stems, webs, grids and honeycombs which, in the later
sixties, became so conspicuous an industry. Both are attempts to avoid
any imputation of prejudice; and if, in the first case, empirical facts are
presumed to be value-free and finally ascertainable, in the second, the
co-ordinates of a grid are awarded an equal impartiality. For, like the lines
of longitude and latitude, it seems to be hoped that these will, in some
way, eliminate any bias—even responsibility—in a specification of the
infilling detail.

But, if the ideally neutral observer is surely a critical fiction, if among
the multiplicity of phenomena with which we are surrounded we
observe what we wish to observe, if our judgements are inherently
selective because the quantity of factual information is finally indigestible,
any literal usage of a 'neutral' grid labours under approximate problems.
The grid is to be either all-encompassing—a practical impossibility, or it
is to be delimited—and hence not neutral; and, therefore, what results
from both 'methodology' and 'systems' (relative to the contexts of facts
and space) can only be the reverse of what was intended—in the one case,
process elevated to the level of icon and, in the other, the covert statement of a tendentious idea.

Which is not to deny the usefulness of well-concerted information
nor the heuristic utility which fantasies of highly organized reality may
often supply; but which is to notice that, by now, the literal extension
of total design into total management and total print out, has, as much
among its proponents as its critics, begun, for some time, to appear as a
rather dubious and fruitless enterprise. And it is perhaps as a result that
there have emerged a series of counter-productions, a barrage of imperfectly defined reactions, not only to the monolithic offensiveness of
would-be systemics but also to its related lack of responsiveness to fine
grain association, immediate circumstance, vitality.

Loosely arranged and somehow attached to this reaction are notions of Ad Hocism, Decentralised Socialism (on the model of the Swiss canton?), the Pop version of townscape and, rather more removed from the architect, versions of advocacy planning, with a whole body of affiliated and allegedly populist strategies—all of them identifiable by a common thread along which they seem to be strung together. That is (and relative to the various 'methodologies' which they would supplant or modify), they, all of them, in one way or another, deal directly with a far more intensive attachment to the elusive predilections of the people. And (again relative to the situation which they have come to find inadequate) these attitudes, by and large, would substitute occasion for space, action for artifact, mobility for fixed meaning and self-generated choice for imposition.

But to maintain this simplification. While much has been done through these attitudes to break down an unmanageable monolith, as a result, there has also been introduced an equally untenable dilemma. For there is surely some question as to the ultimate viability of any wholly popular imperative. *Give 'em what they want*, whether sociologically endorsed or otherwise, has never been a, completely, tenable political dogma; and, to the degree in which they leave this issue unconsidered, these often genuinely modest and disarming revisionist propositions are likely to be found implicated with either or both of two very unpleasant doctrines: *Whatever is is right*—an evidently nauseous idea—and *Vox populi vox dei*—a supposition upon which one might have thought that twentieth century history had already cast a sufficient penumbra of doubt.

The architectural proponents of populism are all for democracy and all for freedom; but they are characteristically unwilling to speculate as to the necessary conflicts of democracy with law, of the necessary collisions of freedom with justice. They address themselves to what they believe to be (and to a large extent are) concrete evils—economic evils, stylistic evils, cultural and ethnic abuse; but they are so much (and often so properly) concerned with specifics as to be typically unable to place libertarian detail in what, for the want of a better world, must be its complementary context of legal and legalistic abstraction. In other words, the populists (like some of the devotees of townscape) are apt to vitiate an entirely plausible argument by their unwillingness to consider the matter of ideal reference; and, because they are likely to be preoccupied with the problem of present minorities, the predicament of the future under-privileged is liable to evade their attention. Suffused with generosity, they surrender to an abstract entity called 'the people'; and, while talking of pluralism (another abstract entity which is usually honoured in the absence of any specific tolerance), they are unwilling to recognize how manifold 'the people' happens to be, and consequently, whatever 'its' will, how much in need of protection from each other its components happen to stand. To date, *Vox populi* takes care of no minorities; and, as for *Whatever is is right* (and isn't just untutored choice splendid!), one can sometimes feel this to be no more than a sociological heat sink, an entirely monstrous conservative plot intended to draw off any possible ebullition of revolutionary steam.

And so, while we have no wish to promote recurrent dualities, versions of the science fiction–townscape confrontation, we find ourselves confronted yet again with the extremes of two positions. There is an abstract, would-be scientific idealism and a concrete, would-be populist empiricism. One discovers one attitude of mind which, whatever it might profess, can scarcely deal with specifics; and one discovers another which, whatever it might need, is radically disinclined to cope with generalities. But, though one must be disposed to wonder why these divisions of humanity should be so, it is also hard not to recognize that the populist revisionists, who are foxes attacking a hedgehog doctrine, precisely because they are attacking this doctrine tend to become hedgehogs themselves. For it is an unfortunate fact that, in proclaiming the primacy of 'the people', there is likely to be constructed a monolith quite as intolerable as any which might result from an insistence upon *the* method and *the* idea.

But, if thus far we seem to have discriminated two alternative prisons for the human spirit and, if one of them is a fortress with electronic controls while the other is an open gaol conducted on compassionate principles (and if we would emphatically prefer to be interned in the second), there are still certain details of imprisonment posturing as liberty which would seem to be common to both of these proposed régimes. And, primarily, these are to be found in an estimation of the future which is roughly shared by both parties alike.

Apparently, and without much divergency of opinion, the future is typically envisaged as some exceptionally delicate embryo enclosed in the womb of the present; and, apparently, and unless we are all very careful, there is far worse than miscarriage which may impend. Indeed to ensure the natural delivery of the future, the present must be rid of all psychological and physiological blockages; and, if this might, frivolously, be called The Doctor Spock Theory of the Future, it is perhaps according to the prescriptions of this theory that the architect confers upon the sociologist the role of cultural obstetrician.

This common myth is patently crisis-ridden; but, if it is the feminine inverse of a more virile stipulation of the same idea (the architect as an athlete in a race with time and technology, beloved of Hannes Meyer and Reyner Banham), in each case the future enters, whether a feeble possibility or a tough growth, as an element to coerce the present. In other words, the future reigns as a, presumably, absolute value; and, because its emergence either must or cannot be impeded, a serious and 'responsible' behaviour becomes enjoined upon us.

Now such fantasies, it should not be necessary to demonstrate, are among the cruder outcroppings of a theory of historical determinism, a sort of *Reader's Digest* version of Hegel which was abundantly taken in by the architectural and planning professions in the earlier years of this century. For certainly at no other time than the present could so many architectural quasi-academics have devoted so much *Sitzfleisch* to the completely extraordinary question: *What shall we do so as to prevent the future from not coming about?*

But, if in previous ages this question can seldom have raised its head (the future being recognized as something which was going to take care of itself anyway), today it is evidently closely involved with even more ingrained presuppositions, with a notion of society as a not-to-be-interrupted vegetable continuum, as a biological or botanical entity, as an animal or plant requiring the most careful and assiduous nurturing. And, if the idea of society as organism is ultimately of classical derivation, and if its nineteenth century refurbishings have already been discussed, and if it may, sometimes, constitute a convenient metaphor, its literal interpretations still evidently involve *we* and *they*. For the animal is presumably to be fed and the plant is to be watered (or else why worry?); and, accordingly, society as a natural organism becomes, in practice, a somewhat domesticated and paternalistic scene. Buildings will proliferate illustrations of growth (rather like specimens in some exotic arboretum); and 'people', just by being 'people', expressing themselves simply in action and, it is hoped, avoiding cerebration, will also help to highlight the spectacle of prosperous vegetation; but it is a well-constructed garden (or zoo) which ensues and it contains no surprises.

It is, sometimes, a little astonishing that the Hegelian conception of progressive dialectic could have reduced itself to anything so disastrously tame, to a situation where growth becomes simply growth in kind, and mere change in size is interpreted as real and intrinsic change. For growth and change, so often confused as one and the same, represent very different aspects of mobility; and the notion of society and culture as simply growth (and therefore change) is a distortion of their essential status as the products of ritual and debate. For ideas and those future ideas which will make the future different from the present (and will, hence, ensure change) simply do not 'grow'. Their mode of existence is neither biological nor botanical. The condition of their being is that of conflict and argument, of consciousness; but, if they emerge through the heat—or the chill—of controversy and through the clash of minds, the residue of historical determinism which we inherit is unwilling to concede anything so obvious.

And, of course, correctly so. For, if one assumes that all ideas are implicit from the beginning of time (like buds awaiting a favourable moment to unfold as flowers) and if one, simultaneously, assumes that all knowledge is accessible (an apparent axiom of 'methodology'), then the irritant and the problem of future ideas will logically vanish away. Simply, since we can now more than intuit them, there will be none; and thus, equipped as we are with the 'laws' of societal and cultural mobility, we shall be enabled smoothly to extrapolate from the *status quo*. Or such is half the story. But, though 'history' and the future are dictatorial, paradoxically and as already noticed, they are usually envisaged as requiring attention; and hence, clearly, the need for the nurture of nature for a species of total design gently but unintermittently applied.

So, perhaps at this stage it is that we reach the final but logical degradation of utopian and millennarian dogma. The new order is to be insidiously and gradually introduced. The technique is to be cultivation and not imposition. The path towards ultimate fulfilment is already disclosed; and, as all cultural markers become increasingly declared oppressive and obsolete so, while we surrender any illusion of free will we may yet retain, we may still be consoled by the faith that such is the way to the rational coherence of libertarian perfection.

This is to exaggerate; but not very greatly. For anyone who chooses to scrutinize the accumulation of inference which contemporary architecture and urbanism fairly readily supplies will, surely, be almost obliged to render some version of the picture we have here painted. 'Growth' assumed to be uninterrupted by politics; total design and total non-design, both equally 'total'; the grid of freedom, assumed to be neutral and natural; the unchecked spontaneity of 'the people', supposed to be equally healthy and independent; the strange collusions between 'science' and 'destiny', between fantasies of authority and fantasies of independence; the choice of skipping around, preferably naked, among the Cartesian co-ordinates or getting gut reactions from the ghetto: the inferences, for the most part, are rather few and very grotesque.

But again, and at the risk of repetition, to proceed from diagnosis to

The fantasy of organic growth—

Candilis, Josic and Woods: project for Toulouse-le-Mirail, 1961

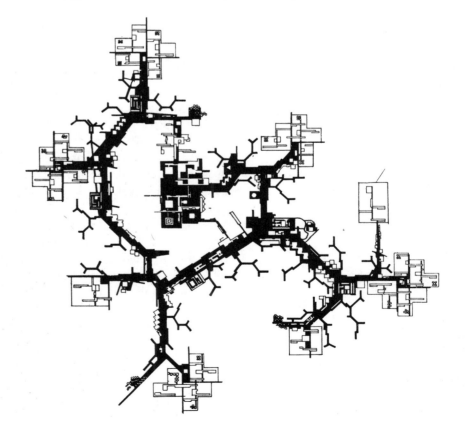

prognosis. The argument which follows involves the surrender or at least, the temporary suspension of a prevalent monocular vision, the willingness to recognize certain fantasies about history and scientific method for the totems which they are, the concession that political process is likely to be neither very smooth nor very predictable and, perhaps above all, the dissolution of a cherished prejudice that all buildings can be, and must become, works of architecture–a prejudice which is, in no way, exactly modified when its resultant proposition is, effectively, turned inside out, i.e. all works of architecture should vanish away.

For, the requirements of professional empire building apart, the demand that all buildings should become works of architecture (or the reverse) is strictly offensive to common sense, If it is possible to define the existential predicament of the art–or whatever–of architecture (and there can be no simple formula implicating bicycle sheds and Lincoln Cathedral), one might possibly stipulate that architecture is a social institution related to building in much the same way that literature is to speech. Its technical medium is public property and, if the notion that all speech should approximate to literature is, *ipso facto*, absurd and would, in practice, be intolerable, much the same may be said about building and architecture. There is no need and no purpose served in insisting that they be identical. Like literature, architecture is a discriminatory concept which can, but need not, enjoy a lively commerce with its vernacular; and, if it should be apparent that nobody is, in any way, seriously the loser by the existence of refined and passionate modes of concatenating words, the value of a parallel activity should scarcely require to be excused.

Growth as a product of conflict and argument–

below
Roman settlement of Aosta

far below
Aosta in the early 19th century

right
The Roman settlement of Timgad, Algeria, with later accretions

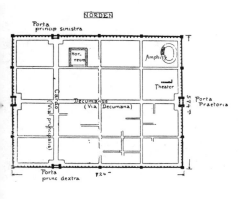

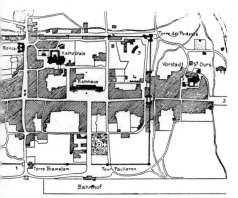

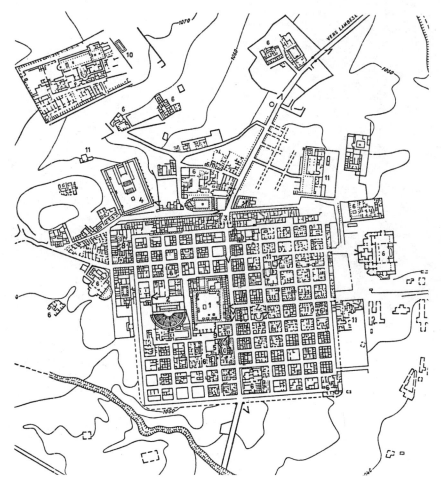

But the exigencies of 'the single central vision', palpitating with the sense of its own goodness, will not allow for any determination so obvious; and, as the architect became both messiah and scientist, both Moses and Newton, the consequences of this role playing were not be evaded. The proofs of legitimacy were to be brought down from an encounter with 'history' on the mountain and, equally, they were to be educed by an observation of no more, and no less, than 'fact'.

However, the myth of the architect as eighteenth century natural philosopher, with all his little measuring rods, balances and retorts (a myth which became all the more ludicrous after its annexation by the architect's less lustrous and less well-pedigreed cousin: the planner), must now be brought into proximity with *The Savage Mind* and with everything that '*bricolage*' represents.

'There still exists among ourselves,' says Claude Lévi-Strauss, 'an activity which on the technical plane gives us quite a good understanding of what a science we prefer to call "prior" rather than "primitive" could have been on the plane of speculation. This is what is commonly called "bricolage" in French;'[9] and he then proceeds to an extended analysis of the objectives of 'bricolage' and of science, of the respective roles of the 'bricoleur' and the engineer.

Rome, Villa Doria-Pamphili, garden structure, window detail

In its old sense the verb 'bricoler' applied to ball games and billiards, to hunting, shooting and riding. It was however always used with reference to some extraneous movement: a ball rebounding, a dog straying or a horse swerving from its direct course to avoid an obstacle. And in our time the 'bricoleur' is still someone who works with his hands and uses devious means compared to those of the craftsman.[10]

Now there is no intention to place the weight of the argument which follows upon Lévi-Strauss's observations. Rather the intention is to promote an identification which may, up to a point, prove useful and, so much so, that if one may be inclined to recognize Le Corbusier as a fox in hedgehog disguise, one may also be willing to envisage a parallel attempt at camouflage: the 'bricoleur' disguised as engineer. 'Engineers fabricate the tools of their time...Our engineers are healthy and virile, active and useful, balanced and happy in their work...our engineers produce architecture for they employ a mathematical calculation which derives from natural law.'[11]

Such is an almost entirely representative statement of early modern architecture's most conspicuous prejudice. But then compare Lévi-Strauss:

The 'bricoleur' is adept at performing a large number of diverse tasks; but, unlike the engineer, he does not subordinate each of them to the availability of raw materials and tools conceived and procured for the purpose of the project. His universe of instruments is closed and the rules of his game are always to make do with 'whatever is at hand', that is to say with a set of tools and materials which is always finite and is also heterogeneous because what it contains bears no relation to the current project, or indeed to any particular project, but is the contingent result of all the occasions there have been to renew or enrich the stock or to

Bricolage–
Rome, Villa Doria-Pamphili,
garden structure

maintain it with the remains of previous constructions or destructions. The set of the 'bricoleur's' means cannot therefore be defined in terms of a project (which would presuppose besides, that, as in the case of the engineer, there were, at least in theory, as many sets of tools and materials, or 'instrumental sets', as there are different kinds of projects. It is to be defined only by its potential use...because the elements are collected or retained on the principle that 'they may always come in handy'. Such elements are specialized up to a point, sufficiently for the 'bricoleur' not to need the equipment and knowledge of all trades and professions, but not enough for each of them to have only one definite. and determinate use. They represent a set of actual and possible relations; they are 'operators', but they can be used for any operations of the same type.[12]

For our purposes it is unfortunate that Lévi-Strauss does not lend himself to reasonably laconic quotation. For the 'bricoleur', who certainly finds a representative in 'the odd job man', is also very much more than this. 'It is common knowledge that the artist is both something of a scientist and of a 'bricoleur';'[13] but, if artistic creation lies mid-way between science and 'bricolage', this is not to imply that the 'bricoleur' is 'backward'. 'It might be said that the engineer questions the universe while the 'bricoleur' addresses himself to a collection of oddments left over from human endeavours;'[14] but it must also be insisted that there is no question of primacy here. Simply, the scientist and the 'bricoleur' are to be distinguished 'by the inverse functions which they assign to event and structures as means and ends, the scientist creating events...by means of structures and the 'bricoleur' creating structures by means of events.'[15]

But we are here, now, very far from the singular notion of an exponential increasingly precise 'science' (a speedboat which architecture

Simulated bricolage—
Luigi Moretti: Rome, Casa del Girasole,
detail

and urbanism are to follow like highly inexpert water-skiers); and, instead, we have not only a confrontation of the 'bricoleur's' 'savage mind' with the 'domesticated' mind of the engineer, but also a useful indication that these two modes of thought are not representatives of a progressive serial (the engineer illustrating a perfection of the 'bricoleur', etc.) but that, in fact, they are necessarily coexistent and complementary conditions of the mind. In other words, we might be about to arrive at some approximation of Lévi-Strauss's 'pensée logique au niveau du sensible'.

There could, of course, have been other routes followed. Karl Popper might have put us down in, very approximately, the same place, Jurgen Habermas might have helped to somewhat equivalent conclusions; but we have preferred Lévi-Strauss because, in his discussion, with its emphasis upon making, it is far more possible for the architect to recognize something of himself. For, if we can divest ourselves of the deceptions of professional *amour propre* and accepted academic theory, the description of the 'bricoleur' is far more of a 'real-life' specification of what the architect-urbanist is and does than any fantasy deriving from 'methodology' and systemics'.

Indeed, one could fear that the architect as 'bricoleur' is, today, almost too enticing a programme—a programme which might guarantee formalism, ad hocery, townscape pastiche, populism and almost what-ever else one chooses to name. But...The savage mind of the bricoleur! The domesticated mind of the engineer/scientist! The interaction of these two conditions! The artist (architect) as both something of a bricoleur and something of a scientist! These evident corollaries should alleviate such fears. However, if the mind of the bricoleur should not be expected to sponsor universal ad hocery, it must still be insisted that the mind of the engineer need not be imagined as supporting the idea of architecture as part of a unified comprehensive science (ideally like physics). And, if Lévi-Strauss's conception of 'bricolage', which patently includes science, may now be placed in some relationship with Popper's conception of science, which evidently excludes 'methodology', there is here the illustration of some more restrictive intention in the present argument. For the predicament of architecture – which, because it is always, in some way or other, concerned with amelioration, by some standard, however dimly perceived, of making things better, with how things ought to be, is always hopelessly involved with value judgements— can never be scientifically resolved, least of all in terms of any simple empirical theory of 'facts'. And, if this is the case with reference to architecture, then, in relation to urbanism (which is not even con-cerned in making things stand up) the question of any scientific resolution of its problems can only become more acute. For, if the notion of a 'final' solution through a definitive accumulation of all data is, evidently, an epistemological chimera, if certain aspects of information will invariably remain undiscriminated or undisclosed, and if the inventory of 'facts' can never be complete simply because of the rates of change and obsolescence, then, here and now, it surely might be possible to assert that *the prospects of scientific city planning should, in reality, be regarded as equivalent to the prospects of scientific politics.*

For, if planning can barely be more scientific than the political society of which it forms an agency, in the case of neither politics nor planning can there be sufficient information acquired before action becomes necessary. In neither case can performance await an ideal future formulation of the problem as it may, at last, be resolved; and, if this is because the very possibility of that future where such formulation might be made depends upon imperfect action now, *then this is only once more to intimate the role of 'bricolage' which politics so much resembles and city planning surely should.*

Indeed, if we are willing to recognize the methods of science and 'bricolage' as concomitant propensities, if we are willing to recognize that they are—both of them—modes of address to problems, if we are willing (and it may be hard) to concede equality between the 'civilized' mind (with its presumptions of logical seriality) and the 'savage' mind (with its analogical leaps), then, in re-establishing 'bricolage' alongside science, it might even be possible to suppose that the way for a truly use-ful future dialectic could be prepared.

A truly useful dialectic?[16] The idea is simply the conflict of contending powers, the almost fundamental conflict of interest sharply stipulated, the legitimate suspicion about others' interests, from which the democratic process—such as it is—proceeds; and then the corollary to this idea is no more than banal: if such is the case, if democracy is compounded of libertarian enthusiasm and legalistic doubt, and if it is, inherently, a collision of points of view and acceptable as such, then why not allow a theory of contending powers (all of them visible) as likely to establish a more ideally comprehensive city of the mind than any which has, *as yet*, been invented.

And there is no more to it than this. In place of an ideal of universal management based upon what are presented as scientific certainties there is also a private, and a public, emancipatory interest (which, incidentally, includes emancipation from management); and, if this is the situation and, if the only outcome is to be sought in collision of interest, in a permanently maintained debate of opposites, then why should this dialectical predicament be not just as much accepted in theory as it is in practice? The reference is again to Popper and to the ideal of keeping the game straight; and it is because, from such a criticist point of view, collision of interest is to be welcomed, not in terms of cheap ecumenicism which is only too abundantly available, but in terms of clarification (because, in the battlefield engendered by mutual suspicion, it is just possible that—as has been usual—the flowers of freedom may be forced from the blood of conflict) that, if such a condition of collisive motives is recognizable and should be endorsable, we are disposed to say: why not try?

The proposition leads us (like Pavlov's dogs) automatically to the condition of seventeenth century Rome, to that collision of palaces, *piazze* and villas, to that inextricable fusion of imposition and accommodation, that highly successful and resilient traffic jam of intentions, an anthology of closed compositions and *ad hoc* stuff in between, which is simultaneously a dialectic of ideal types plus a dialectic of ideal types with empirical context; and the consideration of seventeenth century Rome (the complete city with the assertive identity of its subdivisions: Trastevere, Sant'Eustachio, Borgo, Campo Marzo, Campitelli . . .) leads to the equivalent interpretation of its predecessor where forum and thermae pieces lie around in a condition of inter-dependence, independence and multiple interpretability. And imperial Rome is, of course, far the more dramatic statement. For, certainly with its more abrupt collisions, more acute disjunctions, its more expansive set pieces, its more radically discriminated matrix and general lack of 'sensitive' inhibition, imperial Rome, far more than the city of the High Baroque, illustrates something of the 'bricolage' mentality at its most lavish—an obelisk from here, a column from there, a range of statues from somewhere else, even at the level of detail the mentality is fully exposed; and, in this context, it is amusing to recollect how the influence of a whole school of historians (Positivists, no doubt!) was, at one time, strenuously dedicated to presenting the ancient Romans as inherently nineteenth century engineers, precursors of Gustave Eiffel, who had somehow, and unfortunately, lost their way.

So Rome, whether imperial or papal, hard or soft, is here offered as some sort of model which might be envisaged as alternative to the disastrous urbanism of social engineering and total design. For, while it is recognized that what we have here are the products of a specific topography and two particular, though not wholly separable, cultures, it is also supposed that we are in the presence of a style of argument which is not lacking in universality. That is: while the physique and the politics of Rome provide perhaps the most graphic example of collisive fields and *interstitial debris,* there are calmer versions of equivalent interests which are not hard to find.

Rome, for instance, is—if one wishes to see it so—an imploded version of London. Provide a more bland topography, enlarge the set-pieces and dilute their impact (call the Forum of Trajan, Belgravia and the Baths of Caracalla, Pimlico, for Villa Albani read Bloomsbury and for Via Giulia, Westbourne Terrace) and the works of imperial and papal 'bricolage' will begin to receive their nineteenth century and, more or less, bourgeois analogue—a compilation of rationally gridded fields, mostly corresponding to estate structure, with conditions of confusion and picturesque happening in between, mostly corresponding to stream beds, cow tracks, etc, and, originally serving as a series of inadvertent D.M.Z.'s which could only help to qualify the virtues of order with the values of chaos.

And the Rome—London model may, of course, perfectly well be expanded to provide a comparable interpretation of a Houston or a Los Angeles. It is simply a question of the frame of mind with which one visits a place. That is: if one hopes to find the bizarre it will, perhaps, not elude one's notice and if one hopes to find the way-out future one will, possibly, be equipped to discover it; but, also, if one is looking for the influence of a model, then, within reason, one will probably be enabled to discern its traces. For, in Houston or Los Angeles, if the fields of internal coherence and the areas of interstitial debris are, no doubt, more difficult to identify by explicit name and if their existence we only know by personal exposure, perhaps more important is the tendency in both cities to revert to almost Roman conditions of 'bricolage'. Which is not to assert that simply because a thing is Roman it, just, must be good—we entertain no such fatuous obsession—and which is neither to assert that simply because a thing is Pop-'Roman' it just must be valuable—again we disclaim the intention; but which is, in Houston, to allude to Greenway Plaza, City Post Oak, Plaza del' Ora (hispanicized shades of Tivoli!), Brook Hollow, and, in Los Angeles, to notice their equivalents: local shopping centres, etc., which, if they were not fundamentally apt to be more of the same (more 'modern', more neo-colonial, more dreams of

overleaf
Imperial Rome, views of model at the Museo della Civiltà Romana

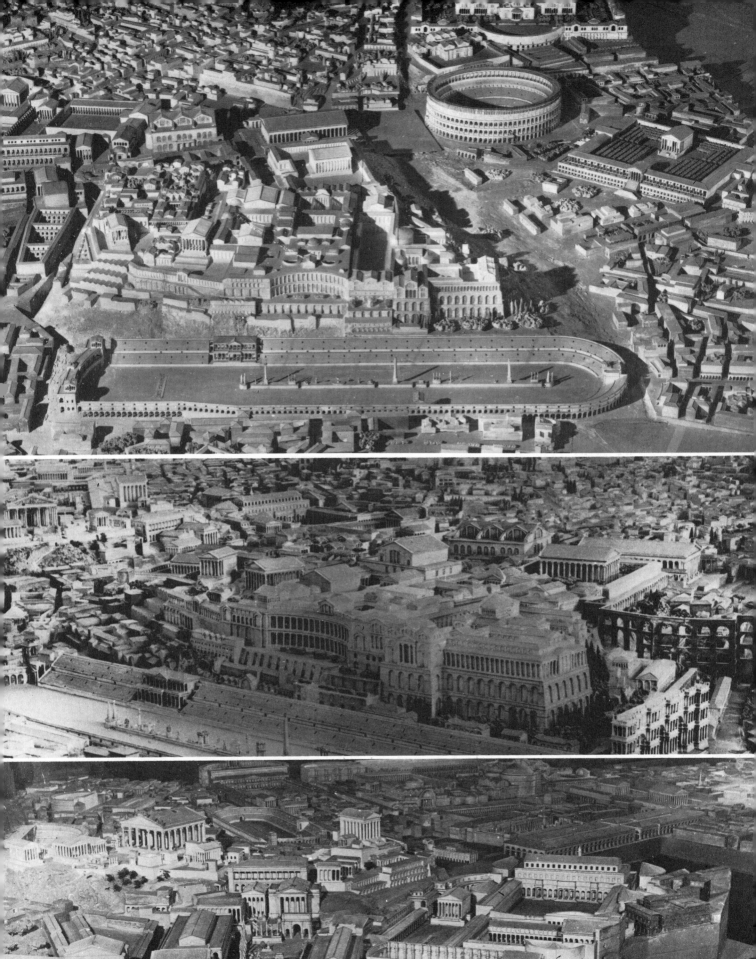

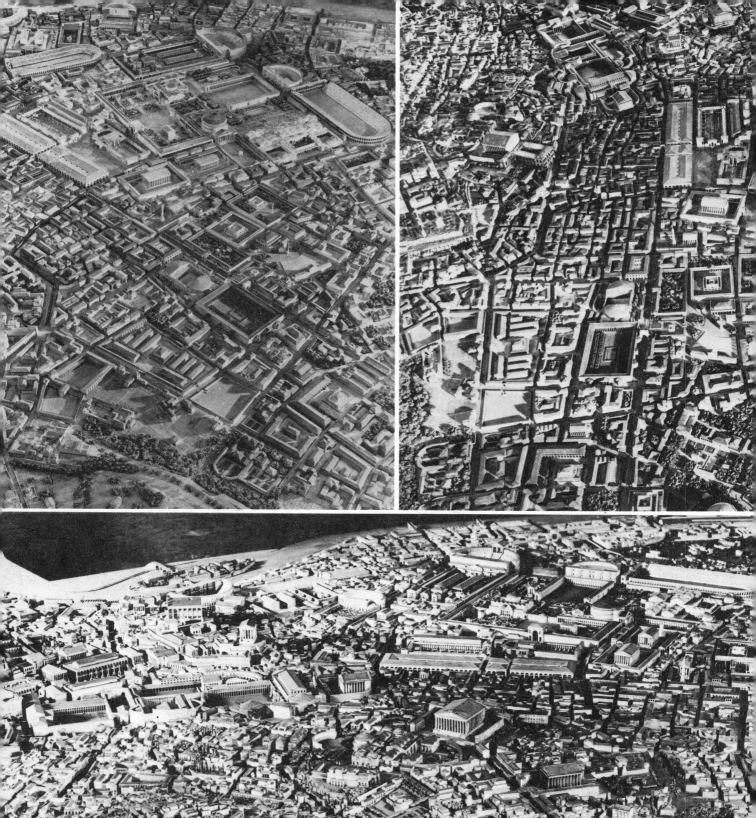

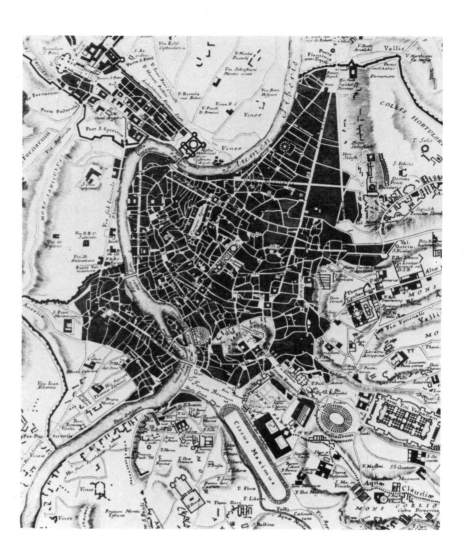

The matrix of 17th century Rome—
plan after Bufalini, 1551

Cordoba) might already be recognized as the equivalent of the great
antique set-pieces.

Admittedly, and to our taste, something may be lost by diffusion,
by the explosive patterns which the automobile has stimulated—collision is not so clearly explicit as one might wish; but, if we do not believe
that the superimposition of rapid transit (after the petroleum is
exhausted?) will, significantly, improve the scene, while we still feel
disposed to salute it as an instance of ongoing 'bricolage', we are also
disposed to imagine that many of the recently enlisted connoisseurs of
Pop (the post-Marxist, post-technophile Banham, the post-elitist
Venturi) have, unconsciously, experienced the same imperative.

However this is to introduce conjecture; and, rather than dwell
upon Rome, London, Houston and Los Angeles as differing versions

of the same paradigm, it might, once more, be useful to return to the Cartesian co-ordinates of happiness, to the neutral grid of equality and freedom—and the reference must be to Manhattan.

Some two thousand blocks were provided, each theoretically two hundred feet wide, no more, no less; and ever since, if a building site was wanted, whether with a view to a church or a blast furnace, an opera house or a toy shop, there is, of intention, no better place in one of these blocks than in another.[17]

But, like all despairing observations, Frederick Law Olmsted's was never completely true. For if, in Manhattan, the unrolling of the blanket grid simultaneously extinguished local detail and illustrated the expertise of the land marketeer in action, it was impossible that the operation could ever be complete. For, while the grid remains belligerently 'neutral' and while its major qualifiers are only to be found on the most general and crude levels (continuous waterfront, Central Park, lower Manhattan, the West Village, Broadway...), in spite of circum-

Imperial Rome, plan after Canina, c.1834

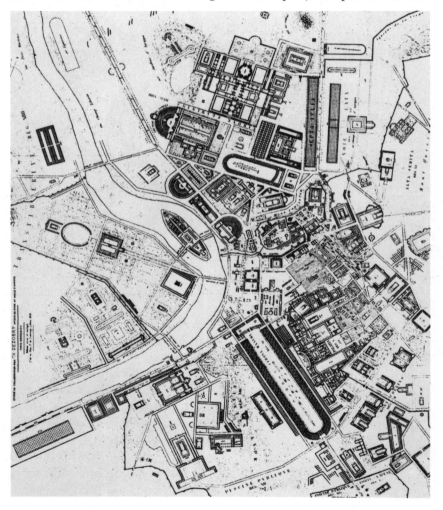

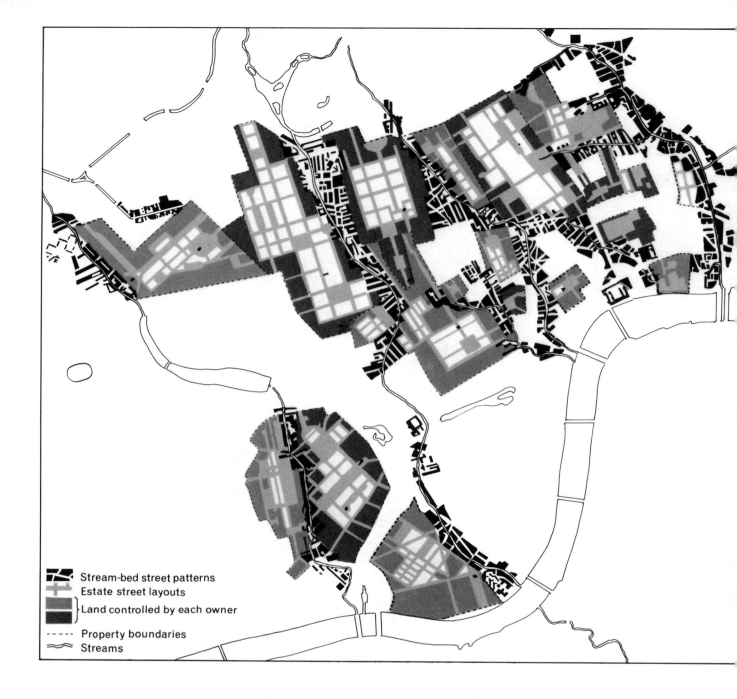

Grahame Shane: field analysis of
central London, 1971

Stream-bed street patterns
Estate street layouts
Land controlled by each owner
- - - - - Property boundaries
~~~ Streams

stance, the evidences of idiosyncratic coagulation present themselves
and demand to be exploited; nor is the situation–which was clearly
visible to Mondrian–one of total defeat. But if, in offering a highly
energetic scaffold for fluctuating and casual event, New York City
might constitute the best of apologias for the all-prevailing grid, the
satisfactions which its grid provides are, perhaps, principally of a conceptual and intellectual order. The, apparently, infinitely extended field,
just as it tends to defeat politics, tends to defeat perception; and it is
presumably in an effort to institutionalize what can only be a felt and a
necessary presence that there have emerged such propositions as 'what

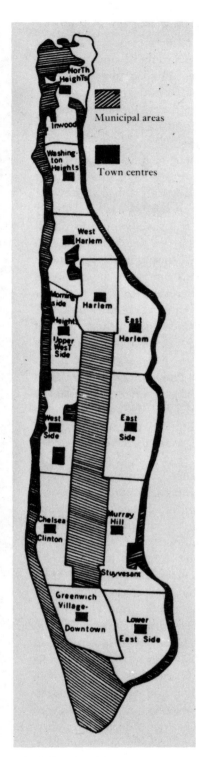

What a democratic Manhattan
would look like, 1973

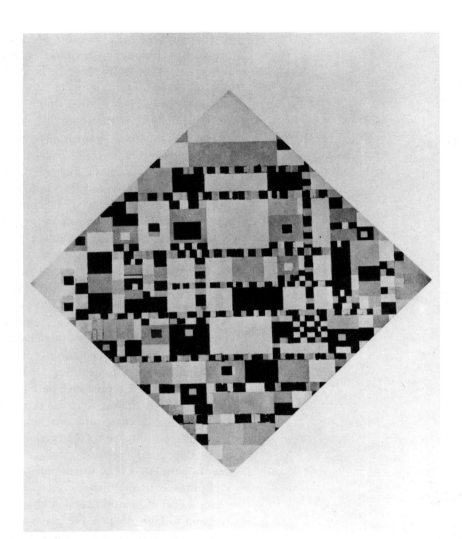

Piet Mondrian: Victory Boogie Woogie,
1943–4

a democratic New York would look like'[18]—demands for the political
cantonization of unrealistically centralized government, demands which,
interestingly, tend to align themselves with what might be the results
of more purely morphological analysis.

Somewhat irrationally the ongoing tradition of modern architecture
would now tend to look with favour upon such proposals as these.
Somewhat irrationally because, however democratic such cantonization
can only appear, the bias which the architect has inherited from long
indulgence of total design fantasies tends to make him incapable of
following through to where such alternative propositions might lead.
For, while there has emerged an awareness of the untenable prospects
of total politics, there remains, or so it would seem, a large lack of
interest or belief in the analogous prospects of any physical counterpart

to such a conclusion. In other words, while in politics the existence of finite fields (interacting with each other but all protected from ultimate infringement) is once more to be considered profitable and desirable, this message seems not, as yet, to have been fully translated into the language of perception; and thus the production of any spatial or temporal equivalent of the finite field is, characteristically, liable to be received with mistrust—again as a blockage of the future and as a dangerous impediment to the freedoms of open-endedness.

Whatever survives of the present argument is now inconsiderable and will carry no conviction whatever for those who, as a basis of operation, are still obliged to conceive of a totally integrated world society, a combination of innate goodness and scientific *savoir faire*, in which all political structures, major or minor, will have become dissolved. We concede the values of this persuasion; but we are also obliged to suggest that the ideally open and emancipated society is not likely to be made this way, that the open society depends upon the complexity of its parts, upon competing group-centred interests which need not be logical but which, collectively, may not only check each other but may, sometimes, also serve as a protective membrane between the individual and the form of collective authority. For the problem should remain that of a tension between quasi-integrated whole and quasi-segregated parts; and, lacking the segregated parts, one can only imagine that 'open society' where, in despite of the theorems of liberty and equality, all the compulsions of fraternity—elective affinities, team sweatshirts, group dynamics, revolutionary communes providing the joys of pleasurable alienation, the Society of Jesus, Lambda Chi, annual conventions, regimental dinners—would break out yet again.

But the issue may, and without extravagance, be equipped with a far more literal illustration; and such words as integration and segregation (related to both politics and perception) can scarcely lead us elsewhere than to the predicament of the American black community. There was, and is, the ideal of integration and there was, and is, the ideal of segregation; but, if both ideals may be supported by a variety of arguments, proper and improper, there remains the evidence that, when gross injustice begins to be removed, the barriers which were formerly maintainable from the outside are just as reconstructable from within. For, whatever fantasies of the ideally open society are maintainable (and Popper's 'open society' may be just as much a fiction as the ideally 'closed society' which he condemns), in spite of the abstract universal goals demanded by theoretical liberalism, there still remains the problem of identity, with its related problems of absorption and extinction of specific type; and it is yet to be proved that such problems should be considered temporary. For the truly empirical order was never liberty, equality, fraternity; but it was rather the reverse: a question of the fraternal order, a grouping of the equal and like-minded, which, collectively, assumes the power to negotiate its freedoms, Such is the history of Christianity,

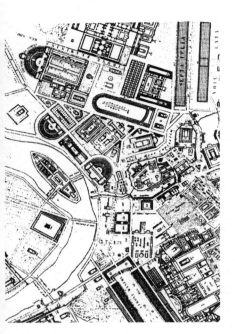

Imperial Rome, plan after Canina,
c. 1834, detail

continental freemasonry, the academic institution, trades' unionism, women's suffrage, bourgeois privilege and all the rest. It is a history of the open field as an idea, the closed field as a fact; and it is because, in this continuous eruption of closed fields which has contributed so much to genuine emancipation, the recent history of black liberties in the United States is so illuminating (and surely so 'correct' in both its aggressive *and* protective attitudes) that we have felt compelled to cite it as a classical—perhaps *the* classical—illustration of a general predicament.

The argument, such as it is, may now be condensed. It certainly concerns the theological extremes of predestination versus free will; and, just as certainly, it is both conservative and anarchistic in its drive. It supposes that, beyond a point, protracted political continuities should neither be postulated nor hoped for and that, correspondingly, the continuities of hyper-extended 'design' should also be viewed with doubt. But it does not suppose that, in the absence of total design merely random procedures can be expected to flourish. Instead, whatever may be the empirical and whatever may be the ideal (and both positions can be distorted by intellectual passion or self-interest to appear their opposites), the ongoing thesis presumes the possibility and the need for a two-way argument between these polar extremes. To a point it is a formalist argument; but, then, to the degree that it contains formalist characteristics, this is not without intention.

'Men living in democratic ages do not readily comprehend the utility of forms.' The date is the early 1830s and the author of the statement is Alexis de Tocqueville who continues:

Yet this objection which the men of democracies make to forms is the very thing which renders forms so useful to freedom; for their chief merit is to serve as a barrier between the strong and the weak, the ruler and the people, to retard the one and to give the other time to look about him. Forms become more necessary in proportion as the government becomes more active and powerful, while private persons are becoming more indolent and feeble...This deserves most serious attention.[19]

And, if it still may deserve at least some attention, it is with such a statement as this, a curiously pragmatic base for a theory of forms, that we again propose the analogue of politics and perception.

To terminate: rather than Hegel's 'indestructible bond of the beautiful and the true', rather than ideas of a permanent and future unity, we prefer to consider the complementary possibilities of consciousness and sublimated conflict; and, if there is here urgent need for both the fox and the 'bricoleur,' perhaps it can only be added that the job ahead should be envisaged as no matter of making the world safe for democracy. It is not totally different; but, certainly, it is not this. For, surely, the job is that of making safe the city (and hence democracy) by large infusions of metaphor, analogical thinking, ambiguity; and, in the face of a prevailing scientism and conspicuous *laissez-aller*, it is just possible that these activities could provide the true *Survival Through Design*.

Collage City
and the Reconquest of Time

Man, in a word, has no nature; what he has is . . . history. Expressed differently: what nature is to things, history, *res gestae*, is to man.

The only radical difference between human history and 'natural' history is that the former can never begin again . . . the chimpanzee and the orangutan are distinguished from man not by what is known strictly speaking as intelligence, but because they have far less memory. Every morning the poor beasts have to face almost total oblivion of what they lived through the day before, and their intellect has to work with a minimum fund of experience. Similarly, the tiger of today is identical with that of six thousand years ago, each one having to begin his life as a tiger from the beginning as if none had existed before him. . . . Breaking the continuity with the past, is a lowering of man and a plagiarism of the orangutan. JOSÉ ORTEGA Y GASSET

This means that you pick up, and try to continue, a line of enquiry which has the whole background of the earlier development of science behind it; you fall in with the tradition of science. It is a very simple and decisive point, but nevertheless one that is not often sufficiently realised by rationalists–that we cannot start afresh; that we must make use of what people have done before us in science. If we start afresh, then, when we die, we shall be about as Adam and Eve were when they died (or, if you prefer, as far as Neanderthal man). In science we want to make progress, and this means that we must stand on the shoulders of our predecessors. We must carry on a certain tradition. . . .
KARL POPPER

right
Rome, the oculus of the Pantheon

below
a mandala

To move now from the consideration of a collision of physical constructs to the further consideration of collision, this time on a psychological and, to some degree, a temporal plane. The city of collisive intentions, however much it may be presentable in terms of pragmatics, is evidently also an icon, and a political icon signifying a range of attitudes relating to historical process and social change. So much should be obvious. But, if Collision City, as so far discussed, has only incidentally betrayed an iconic intention, questions of symbolic purpose or function begin now increasingly to rise to the surface.

For one mode of thought it is a psychological necessity that things are what they are; for another something like the reverse is true: things are never what they seem to be and the phenomenon always disguises its own essence. For the one state of mind facts are readily ascertainable, concrete and always susceptible to laconic description. For the other facts are essentially fugitive and will never yield themselves to specification. The one intellectual party requires the supports of definition, the other the illuminations of interpretation; but, if neither attitude enjoys a monopoly of empirical understanding or idealist fantasy, their characterization need not be unduly prolonged. Both mental conditions are only too familiar; and, if it is all too simple (and not completely accurate) to speak of the one attitude as iconoclast and the other as iconophile, it is just such an elementary distinction that is here proposed.

Iconoclasm is and should be an obligation. It is the obligation to expurgate myth and to break down intolerable conglomerates of meaning; but, if one may perfectly well sympathize with the type of the Goth and the Vandal in his efforts to free the world from a stifling excess of reference, one is also obliged to recognize the ultimate uselessness—in terms of original intentions—of any such endeavours. Temporarily they may induce elation, self-gratification and a whole release of hyper-thyroid excitements; but permanently—and as one knows—such efforts can only contribute to yet another iconography. For, if one can agree with Ernst Cassirer and the many of his following[1] that no human gesture can be wholly free from symbolic content, this is only to acknowledge that, while we go through all the public motions of expelling myth through the front door, then, even while (and because) we are doing so, myth is still effecting an insidious re-entry via the kitchen. We may claim rationality. We may insist that reason is always simply reasonable—no more and no less; but a certain stubborn totemic *matériel* will still refuse to go away. For, to iterate Cassirer's primary intuition, however much we may aspire to logic, we are still confronted with the circumstance that language, the prime instrument of thought, inevitably antedates and casts a cloud over all elementary programmes of simple logical procedure.

It has been the splendour and the tragic limitation of the revolutionary tradition to have disregarded (or to have affected to disregard) this predicament. Revolutionary light will banish obscurity. With the revolution achieved human affairs will become located in the full radiance of enlightenment. Such, again and again, has been the revolutionary presumption; and, deriving from it, again and again there has ensued an almost predictable disillusion. For, whatever the abstract height of the rational project, the totemic stuff has simply refused to be expunged. Merely it has discovered for itself a new disguise; and in this way, concealing itself in the sophistications of freshly invented camouflage, it has invariably been enabled to operate quite as effectively as ever.

Such has been the history of twentieth century architecture and urbanism: the overt expulsion of all deleterious cultural fantasy and the simultaneous proliferation of fantasy not conceived to be such. On the one hand, the building and the city were to advertise no more than a scientifically determined pattern of performance and efficiency; but, on the other, as the evidence of a complete integration of subject and content, either imminent or already achieved, they could only be charged with an emblematic role. Their covert purpose was sententious; they preached; and indeed so much so that, if one must think of the city as inherently a didactic instrument, then the city of modern architecture will surely long survive in the critical literature of urbanism as a prime illustration of an irrepressible tendency to edify.

The city as didactic instrument. It is not then a question as to whether it should be so. It is rather a matter that it cannot be otherwise. And, this being so, it is therefore a question of the nature of the instructive information which is deliverable, of approximately how a desirable discourse is to be formulated, of what criteria are to determine the city's preferred ethical content.

Now this is an issue involving the highly uncertain roles of custom and innovation, of stability and dynamism, of—in the end—coercion and emancipation which it would be happiness to evade; but the lines of the much travelled escape routes—'Let science build the town', 'Let people build the town'—have already been delineated and dismissed. For, if an allegedly cool rationale of 'facts' and numbers may disclose an ethical tissue full of dubieties, may justify not only the city of deliverance but also the moral catastrophes of an Auschwitz or a Vietnam, and if the lately resurrected 'power to the people' can only be preferred to this, this too cannot be without massive qualification. Nor, in the context of a model city, a city of the mind, can simply functional or simply formal preoccupations be allowed to suppress questions relating to the style and substance of discourse.

Which is to notice that in the arguments which follow it is supposed that, in a final analysis, there are only two reservoirs of ethical content available for our use. *These are: tradition and utopia, or whatever intimations of significance our notions of tradition and utopia may still provide.* These, whether separately or together, positive or negative, have been the ultimate servicing agents of all the various cities of 'science' and 'people', of 'nature' and 'history' already noticed; and, since there is no doubt that, practically, they have acted as a very coherent litmus of action and reaction (perhaps the most coherent of any) they are here cited as final, though far from absolute, references.

This is not entirely to proclaim paradox. We have already stated reservations about utopia. We shall go on to stipulate reservations about tradition; but it would be facetious further to indulge speculation in this area without first directing some attention to the still insufficiently regarded evaluations of Karl Popper.[2] Popper, the theorist of scientific method who believes that objective discernible truth is not available, who proposes the necessity of conjecture and the subsequent obligation towards every degree of refutation, is also the Viennese liberal long domiciled in England and using what appears to be a Whiggish theory of the state as criticism of Plato, Hegel and, not so incidentally, of the Third Reich. The *philosophe engagé*, dedicated via experience to attack upon all doctrines of historical determinism and all assumptions of the closed society: it is in terms of this background that Popper, the apostle of scientific rigour, further presents himself as the critic of utopia and the exponent of tradition's usefulness; and it is in these identical terms that he may also be seen to emerge as, by implication, the greatest of critics of modern architecture and urbanism (though in practice it might be doubted whether he possesses the technical capacity, or the interest, to criticize either).

So Popper's theory of traditional value may seem, logically, to be unfaultable; and it may also seem, emotionally, to be unpalatable. Tradition is indispensable–communication rests upon tradition; tradition is related to a felt need for a structured social environment; tradition is the critical vehicle for the betterment of society; the 'atmosphere' of any given society is connected with tradition: and tradition is somewhat akin to myth, or–to say it in other words–specific traditions are somehow incipient theories which have the value, however imperfectly, of helping to explain society.

But such statements also require to be placed alongside the conception of science from which they derive: the largely anti-empirical conception of science not so much as the accumulation of facts but as the criticism, in terms of their non-performance, of hypotheses. It is hypotheses which discover facts and not vice versa; and, seen in this way–so the argument runs–the role of traditions in society is roughly equivalent to that of hypotheses in science. That is: just as the formulation of hypotheses or theories results from the criticism of myth,

Similarly traditions have the important double function of not only creating a certain order or something like a social structure, but also of giving us something on which we can operate; something that we can criticise and change. (And)...just as the invention of myth or theories in the field of natural science has a function–that of helping us to bring order into the events of nature–so has the creation of traditions in the field of society.[3]

And it is, presumably, for such reasons that a rational approach to tradition becomes contrasted by Popper with the rationalist attempt to transform society by the agency of abstract and utopian formulations. Such attempts are 'dangerous and pernicious'; and, if utopia is 'an attractive...an all too attractive idea', for Popper it is also 'self-defeating and it leads to violence'. But again to condense the argument:

1. It is impossible to determine ends scientifically. There is no scientific way of choosing between two ends....
2. The problem of constructing a utopian blue print (therefore) cannot possibly be solved by science alone....
3. Since we cannot determine the ultimate ends of political actions

scientifically ... they will at least partly have the character of religious differences. And there can be no tolerance between these different utopian religions ... the utopianist must win over or else crush his competitors.... But he has to do more ... (for) the rationality of his political action demands constancy of aim for a long time ahead....
4. The suppression of competing aims becomes even more urgent if we consider that the period of utopian construction is liable to be one of social change. (For) in such a time ideas are liable to change also. (And) thus what may have appeared to many as desirable when the utopian blue print was decided upon may appear less desirable at a later date....
5. If this is so, the whole approach is in danger of breaking down. For if we change our ultimate political aims while attempting to move towards them we may soon discover that we are moving in circles ... (and) it may easily turn out that the steps so far taken lead in fact away from the new aim....
6. The only way to avoid such changes of our aims seems to be to use violence, which includes propaganda, the suppression of criticism, and the annihilation of all opposition.... The utopian engineers must in this way become omniscient as well as omnipotent.[4]

It is perhaps unfortunate in all this that Popper makes no distinction between utopia as metaphor and utopia as prescription; but, if he is evidently concerned with the scrutiny—in terms of their probable practical results—of certain largely unthinking procedures and attitudes, the intellectual situation which he has felt persistently compelled to review is comparatively easy to exhibit.

The announcement by the White House on 13 July 1968 of the creation of the National Goals Research Staff stated the following:

There are increasing numbers of forecasting efforts in both public and private institutions, which provide a growing body of information upon which to base judgements of probable future developments and of choices available.

There is an urgent need to establish a more direct link between the increasingly sophisticated forecasting now done and the decision making process. The practical importance of establishing such a link is emphasised by the fact that virtually all the critical national problems of today could have been anticipated well in advance of their reaching critical proportions.

An extraordinary array of tools and techniques has been developed by which it becomes increasingly possible to project future trends—and thus to make the kind of informed choices which are necessary if we are to establish mastery over the process of change.

These tools and techniques are gaining widespread use in the social and physical sciences, but they have not been applied systematically and comprehensively to the science [sic] of government. The time is at hand when they should be used and when they must be used.[5]

'The science of government', 'tools and techniques' which 'must be used', 'sophisticated forecasting', 'the kind of informed choices which are necessary if we are to establish mastery over the process of change': this is Saint-Simon and Hegel, the myths of potentially rational society and inherently logical history installed in the most unlikely of high places; and, in its naïvely conservative but simultaneously neo-Futurist tone, as a popular rendition of what is by now folk lore, it might almost have been designed as a target for Popper's critical strategies. For, if 'mastery over the process of change' may indeed sound heroic, the strict lack of sense of this idea can only be emphasized; and, if this is the simple fact that 'mastery over the process of change' would necessarily eliminate all but the most minor and extrinsic changes, then such is the real burden of Popper's position. Simply that, in so far as the form of the future depends upon future ideas this form is not to be anticipated; and that, therefore, the many future-oriented fusions of utopianism and historicism (the ongoing course of history to be subject to rational management) can only operate to restrain any progressive evolution, any genuine emancipation.

And perhaps it may be at this point that one does distinguish the quintessential Popper, the libertarian critic of historical determinism and strictly inductivist views of scientific method who surely more than anyone else has probed and discriminated that crucial complex of historico-scientific fantasies which, for better or worse, has been so active a component of twentieth century motivation.

But we here approach Popper, who it has already been suggested is—inferentially—the most completely devastating critic of almost everything which the overtly twentieth century city has represented, with the anxiety to salvage at least *something* from the results of his analysis. We approach him, that is, with some of the surviving prejudices (or from the traditional point of view) of what used to be called the modern movement; and our own disagreements with his position are comparatively easy to state. Briefly: his evaluations of utopia and tradition seem to present irreconcilable styles of critical involvement; the one is heated, the other cool, and his distinctly abrupt denunciations of utopia are slightly less than pleasing when they are brought into conjunction with the sophistications of his endorsement of tradition. Apparently much can be forgiven tradition; but, if nothing can be forgiven utopia, one may still feel disturbed by this evidence of special pleading. For the abuses of tradition are surely not any less great than the abuses of utopia; and, if one may feel obliged to concede the accuracy of Popper's condemnation of a prescriptive utopia, one may also ask: *How is it that, if enlightened traditionalism may be distinguished from blind traditionalist faith, the concept of utopia cannot be comparably articulated?*

For, if Popper is able to attribute a sort of proto-theoretical status to tradition and if he is able to envisage social progress as ensuing from a continuous criticism of tradition, that he cannot make these accommodations with reference to utopia can only be considered unhappy.

Utopia has achieved great universality by evincing great understanding and sympathy with all men. Like tragedy it deals with the ultimates of good and evil, virtue and vice, justice and continence and the judgement that is to come. The whole is suffused with two of the tenderest of all human feelings: pity and hope.[6]

But Popper, with his admirable condemnation of political excess, finding literal utopia to promise nothing more than sociological nightmare, seems deliberately to render himself obtuse to the promptings of that great body of manifestations which, particularly in the arts, the myth of the absolutely good society has engendered. He condemns utopian politics and seems unprepared to make any accommodation of utopian poetics. The open society is good, the closed society is bad; therefore utopia is bad and let us have no thought for its by-products. Such would seem to be a very crude digest of his position which we would wish to qualify in the following terms: utopia is embedded in a mesh of ambiguous political connotations and this is to be expected; but, since utopia is something perhaps by now ingrained (and certainly ingrained in the Hebreo-Christian tradition), it cannot, and should not, be something wholly made to go away. A political absurdity, it might remain a psychological necessity. Which, translated into architectural terms, could be a statement concerning the ideal city—for the most part physically insufferable, but often valuable to the degree that it may involve some kind of dimly perceived conceptual necessity.

But, if Popper's rejection of utopia (while he seems surreptitiously to posit a tacit utopian condition in which all citizens are involved in rational dialogue, in which the accepted social ideal is that of a Kantian self-liberation through knowledge) might seem strange, the twentieth century architect's comparable rejection of tradition (while, not so surreptitiously, he maintains a tacit affiliation to what is by now a distinctly traditional body of attitudes and procedures) is surely more explicable. For if, as Popper has surely demonstrated, tradition is unavoidable, then, among the definitions of the word, there is one to which traditionalists do not often refer. A tradition is 'a giving up, surrender, betrayal'. More particularly it is 'a surrender of sacred books in times of persecution'; and this involvement of tradition with treachery is quite possibly some deeply rooted thing which is given in the origins of language. *Traduttore-traditore*, translator-traitor, *traiteur-traité*, traitor-treaty: in these senses the traditionalist traitor is always that person who has abandoned a purity of intention in order to negotiate meanings and principles, perhaps ultimately to treat or to trade with hostile circumstances. An etymology which is eloquently indicative of social prejudice. By the standards of aristocratic, military, or merely intellectual rationalism the traditionalist, in these terms, ranks very low. He corrupts and he accommodates; he prefers survival to the intransigence of ideas, the oases of the flesh to the deserts of the spirit; and, if not criminally feeble, his capacities for the most part are at the level of the mercantile and the diplomatic.

These are among the aspects of tradition which explain the twentieth century architect's loudly paraded distaste for it; but, if much the same distaste may also be felt for utopia (though it has rarely been felt by the architect), these largely uncritical or all-encompassing reactions have, in some way, to be overcome. For, in the end (or so it is here assumed), one is still obliged to struggle with the manifold emanations, legitimate and illegitimate, positive and negative, of both tradition *and* utopia.

But to introduce a concrete illustration of the problem (not wholly unlike the problem of today) which is presented by a utopia in which one has ceased completely to believe and a tradition from which one is critically detached. Napoleon I entertained the project of turning Paris into a species of museum. The city was, to some degree, to become a sort of habitable exhibition, a collection of permanent reminders which were to edify both the resident and the visitor; and the substance of the instruction, one guesses right away, was to be some kind of historical panorama not only of the greatness and continuity of the French nation but, also, of the comparable (though surely slightly less) contributions of a mostly subservient Europe.[7]

So, instinctively one recoils from the idea; but, if it must for the present day command something less than enthusiasm (one is apt to think of Albert Speer and his unfortunate sponsor), one is still, with Napoleon's idea, presented with the fantasy of a great emancipator, still provided with the embryonic programme for what, in its day, could be regarded as a genuinely radical gesture. For this is perhaps one of the first appearances of what was to be a recurrent, and maybe not a repressive, nineteenth century theme: the city as museum.

The city as museum, the city as a positive concert of culture and educational purpose, the city as a benevolent source of random but carefully selected information, was perhaps to be most abundantly realized in the Munich of Ludwig I and Leo von Klenze, in that Biedermayer Munich with its supremely conscientious profusion of

Leo von Klenze: Munich, Propylaen, 1846-60

The Munich of Ludwig I and Leo von
Klenze, model by L. Seitz

references—Florentine, medieval, Byzantine, Roman, Greek—all of them
looking like so many plates from Durand's *Précis des Leçons*. But, if
the idea of this city, which seems to have found its time in the decade of
the 1830s, is surely implicit in the cultural politics of the early nineteenth
century, its significance has remained unassessed.

One observes the evidences of Von Klenze's Munich, one adds traces
of Schinkelesque Potsdam and Berlin, maybe one provincializes the
scene by the notice of such a small Piedmontese city as Novara (scattered
around there might be several such), one then proceeds to incorporate
instances, a little late, of the best French quality (Bibliothèque Ste.
Geneviève, etc.) and gradually retarded aspects of the Napoleonic
dream begin to assume substance. Self-conscious beyond a doubt, the
city as museum is distinguishable from the city of Neo-Classicism by its
multi-formity; and, in its greatest clarity, it scarcely survives beyond
1860. The Paris of Haussmann and the Vienna of the Ringstrasse are

facing page
top left
Leo von Klenze: Munich, Hauptpost, 1836

second from top left
Munich, Odeonsplatz with the Feldherrn-Halle of Friedrich von Gärtner, 1841-4

third from top left
Leo von Klenze: Munich, Residenz, Allerheiligenhofkirche, 1826-37, and Apothekerflügel, 1832-42

below
Leo von Klenze: Munich, Ludwigstrasse, 1842

top right
Leo von Klenze: Munich, Allerheiligenhofkirche, 1826-37

no more than the corruptions of this picture. For already by then—and particularly in Paris—the ideal of a conglomerate of independent parts has again become replaced by the far more 'total' vision of absolute continuity.

But, if this is some attempt to identify the city as museum, the city of precisely presented discrete objects/episodes, then what to say about it? That, in mediating the residue of classical decorum and the incipient optimism of the liberal impulse, it operates as interim strategy? That, though its instructive mission is paramount, it addresses itself to 'culture' rather than technology? That it still incorporates both Brunelleschi *and* the Crystal Palace? That neither Hegel, Prince Albert nor Auguste Comte were strangers to this city?

These are all questions which the equivocal and eclectic conception of city as museum (the first sketch for the city of a ruling bourgeoisie?) may elicit; and they are probably all to be answered in the affirmative. For whatever our reservations (this city is a rattling of dead bones, a mere anthology of historical and picturesque high spots), it is difficult

Leo von Klenze: Munich, Odeonsplatz, project for a monument to the Bavarian army, 1818; to the right, his Leuchtenberg-Palais, 1816-21; left, his Odeon, 1826-8. A version of this obelisk was later erected in the Karolinenplatz, 1833

The Munich of Ludwig I and Leo von
Klenze, model by L. Seitz in the
Munich Nationalmuseum

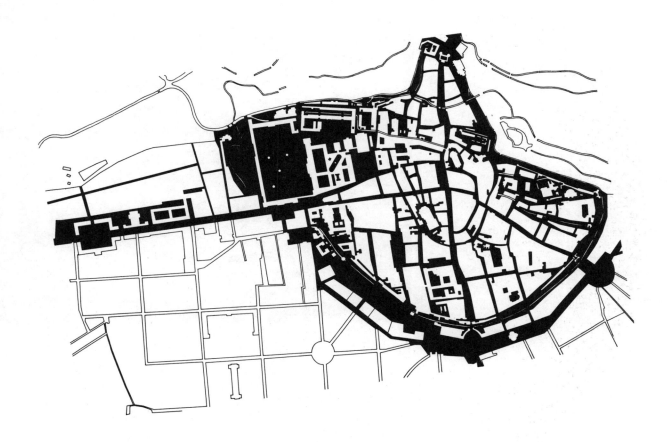

Munich, c.1840, figure-ground plan

right
P. Speeth: Wurzburg, women's
penitentiary, 1800

far right Paris, Galerie d'Orléans, c.1830

far right centre
London, circular engine-house, Camden
Town depot, North Western Railway,
1847

far right below
Karl Friedrich Schinkel: Berlin, Palais
Redern, 1832

not to concede its amiability and its hospitality. An open city and, to a
degree, a critical one, receptive–in theory at least–to the most disparate
stimuli, hostile to neither utopia nor tradition, while by no means
value free the city as museum discloses no intimations of urgent belief
in the value of any all-validating principle. The reverse of restrictive,
implying the entertainment rather than the exclusion of the manifold,
by the standards of its day it surrounds itself with the minimum of
customs barriers, of embargoes, of restraints upon trade; and, accordingly, the *idea* of the city as museum, felicitous in spite of many valid
objections, may, today, be not so readily dismissible as one at first
imagines. For, if the city of modern architecture, open though it has
always professed to be, has displayed a lamentable lack of tolerance for
any import foreign to itself (open field and closed mind), if its basic
posture has been protectionist and restrictive (tight controls to stimulate

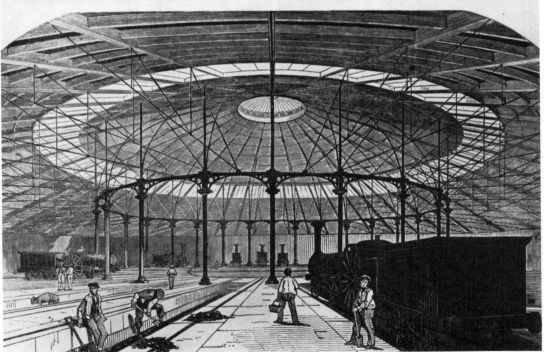

more of the same), and if this has resulted in a crisis of internal economy (increasing poverty of meaning and decline of invention), then the presumptions of formerly unquestionable policy can no longer provide any plausible framework for exclusion.

Which is scarcely to suggest that the Napoleonic city as museum offers any rapidly exploitable model for the solution of all the problems of the world; but which should be to imply that this particular city of nineteenth century wish fulfilment—an assemblage of Greek and Italian mementoes, of a few Nordic fragments, of a sporadic technophile enthusiasm, of maybe a brief flirtation with the Saracenic remains of Sicily—though to us it may seem a claustrophobic and dated little collection, might be regarded as a miniature anticipation of problems not entirely unlike our own: disintegration of absolute conviction, random and 'freely' operating susceptibility, inevitable multiplicity of reference and all the rest. As anticipation and as not wholly inadequate response: for the city as museum, like the museum itself, is a concept embedded in Enlightenment culture, in the information explosion of the later eighteenth century; and, if this explosion has, to date, only increased in both range and impact, it is not very clear that twentieth century attempts to cope with the fall out have been any more successful that those of more than a hundred years ago.

In Berlin a Marx-Engels Platz, in Chicago an Eisenhower Expressway, in Paris an Avenue Général Leclerc, and outside London a Brunel University, all of them corroborate a memorial intention both blatant and indispensable; but, if all of these—by inciting themes of routine recollection—belong to a version of the Napoleonic museum, at a more recondite level one is further confronted with the architect's own working collection—Mykonos, Cape Canaveral, Los Angeles, Le Corbusier, the Tokyo Cabinet, the Constructivist Room and the obligatory West African Gallery (to be finally ceded to us by the Museum of 'Natural' History)—which, in its way, is yet another anthology of commemorative gestures.

Now which of these aggressive public testimonials or which of these private architectural fantasies is the more oppressive, or alternatively, the more representative, is hard to say. But, if all these tendencies present an enduring problem, spatial and temporal, to the ideal of institutionalized neutrality, then this is the problem with which we are concerned: the problem of neutrality, of that ultimately classical ideal

left
Leo von Klenze: Munich, Glaspalast, 1854

above
Luigi Canina: Rome, Villa Borghese, gates from the Piazzale Flaminio, 1825-8

right top
Anon.: Florence, Palazzo 'Der Villa', c.1850

right below
Gustav Albert Wegmann: Zurich, Grossmünster School, 1850-3

far right below
Friedrich von Gärtner: Munich, staircase of the Staatsbibliothek, 1832

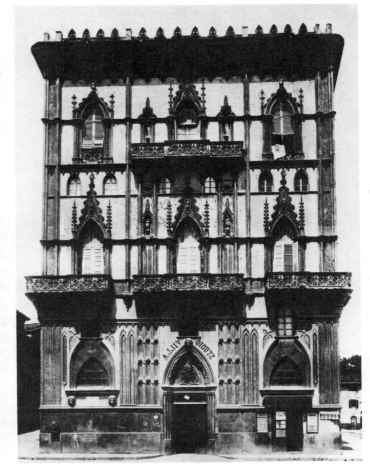

which has long been deprived of classical substance, and of its inevitable infiltration by diversity, by the irrepressible and accelerating accidents of space and time, preference and tradition. The city as a neutral and comprehensive statement, the city as an *ad hoc* representation of cultural relativism; an attempt has been made to identify the protagonists of both these, more or less, exclusive positions; and, in trying to give substance to a city of Napoleonic imagination, some skeletal outline of what seems to have been a nineteenth century attempt to mediate a comparable though less aggravated condition has been presented. As a public institution the museum emerged consequent to the collapse of classical visions of totality and in relation to the great cultural revolution which is most dramatically signified by the political events of 1789. It came into existence in order to protect and display a plurality of physical manifestations representing a plurality of states of mind–all assumed to be in some degree valuable; and, if its evident functions and pretensions were liberal, if the concept of museum therefore implied some kind of ethical ballast, hard to specify but inherent in the institution itself (again the emancipation of society through self-knowledge?), if, to repeat, it was a mediating concept, then it is in terms analogous to the museum that one might postulate a possible solution for the more eminent problems of the contemporary city.

It is suggested that the museum predicament, a predicament of culture, is not readily to be overcome; it is further suggested that its overt presence is more readily to be tolerated than its surreptitious influence; and it is obviously recognized that the designation 'city as museum' can only be repulsive to contemporary sensibility. The designation *city as scaffold for exhibition demonstration* almost certainly introduces a more palatable terminology; but, whichever designation is the more useful, both of them in the end are faced with the issue of museum–scaffold versus exhibits–demonstrations; and, depending upon the working up of the show, this can first lead to two major questions. Does the scaffold dominate the exhibits? Or do the exhibits overwhelm the scaffold?

This is a matter of Lévi-Strauss's precarious balance: 'between structure and event, necessity and contingency, the internal and the external–constantly threatened by forces which act in one direction or the other according to fluctuation in fashion, style and general social conditions;[8]' and, in general, modern architecture resolved its understanding of these questions in favour of an all-pervasive scaffold which largely exhibited itself, a scaffold which pre-empted and controlled any incidentals. This being the case, one also knows, or can imagine, the the opposite condition in which the exhibits take over, even to the degree of the scaffold being driven underground or wished away (Disney World, the American romantic suburb, etc.). But, apart from these alternatives which both exclude the possibilities of competition, if the scaffold tends to simulate necessity and the exhibited object freedom, if one of them might simulate utopia and the other tradition, there remains the obligation–for those who are predisposed to envisage architecture as dialectic–further to conceive of a two-way commerce between scaffold and object, 'structure' and 'event', between the fabric of the museum and its contents, a commerce in which both components retain an identity enriched by intercourse, in which their respective roles are continuously transposed, in which the focus of illusion is in constant fluctation with the axis of reality.

'I have never made trials nor experiments,' 'I can hardly understand the importance given the word research,' 'Art is a lie which makes us realize the truth, at least the truth it is given us to understand,' 'The artist must know the manner of convincing others of the truthfulness of his lies.' With such statements as these of Picasso's[9] one might be reminded of Coleridge's definition of a successful work of art as that which encourages 'a willing suspension of disbelief' (it might also be the definition of a successful political achievement). The Coleridgean mood may be more English, more optimistic, less drenched with Spanish irony; but the drift of thought–the product of an apprehension of reality as far from tractable–is much the same: and, of course, as soon as one begins to think of things in this way, everyone but the most entrenched pragmatist gradually becomes very far removed from the advertised state of mind and the happy certainties of what is sometimes described as modern architecture's 'mainstream'. For one now enters a territory from which the architect and the urbanist have, for the most part, excluded themselves. The vital mood is now completely transformed. One is no less in the twentieth century; but the blinding self-righteousness of unitary conviction is at last placed alongside a more tragic cognition of the dazzling and the scarcely to be resolved multeity of experience.

Which may be to recognize that, unobserved, mostly ignored by the architect, there have long been available two distinct but interrelated formulations of modernity. There is the formulation, dominant for the architect, which might be described by the names: Emile Zola, H.G. Wells, Marinetti, Walter Gropius, Hannes Meyer; and there is the alternative formulation which could be indentified by the further names: Picasso, Stravinsky, Eliot, Joyce, possibly Proust. So far as we are aware this very obvious comparison of two traditions has never been made; and, having produced it, we are arrested by the imbalance of poverty on the one side and richness on the other. We would wish to equip the comparison with at least some degree of symmetry. We would prefer that these two formulations be of equal profundity; and therefore we ask, and with anxiety, whether it must indeed be assumed that the serious strivings of honest anonymity (an ideal in the architect's tradition) are so very much more important than the enlightened findings of sensitized intuition. We ask if this is likely, if it can even be fair; and, paraphrasing Yeats, we also wonder whether really it might be true that 'the best lack all conviction while the worst are full of passionate intensity'. In any case we are disturbed. For the comparison, although it may be contrived, reveals, in one of its parts, a provincialism which, in even the most charitable observer, might stimulate dismay.

The two formulations of modernity which now elaborate themselves are already more or less characterized; but into this situation there must yet again be intruded the Marxian conversion of Hegel's spiritual essence into material substance—a conversion at once valuable, disastrous and creative for modern architecture. For it is surely this and parallel contributions to a singular conception of history, science, society and production (Darwin plus Marx, Wagner and the Gesamtkunstwerk), a conception often supposing itself to be value free and generally presuming its values to be self-evident—which so readily enters into alliance with the common-sense (and commonplace) values of a matter of fact empiricism which, when ignited by millennialistic excitement, constitutes the architect's tradition of modernity; and it is against this very restrictive and indeed superstitious approach to problems that there are now suggested the far less prejudiced techniques of what is, after all, a highly visible and central attitude.

The tradition of modern architecture, always professing a distaste for art, has characteristically conceived of society and the city in highly conventional artistic terms—unity, continuity, system; but the alternative and apparently far more 'art'-prone method of procedure has, so far as one can see, never felt any need for such literal alignment with 'basic' principles. The alternative and predominant tradition of modernity has always made a virtue of irony, obliquity and multiple reference. We think of Picasso's bicycle seat (Bull's Head) of 1944:

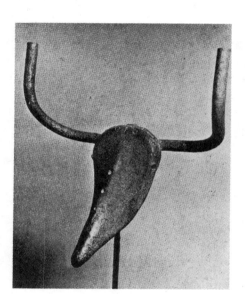

Picasso: Bull's head, 1944

You remember that bull's head I exhibited recently? Out of the handlebars and the bicycle seat I made a bull's head which everybody recognized as a bull's head. Thus a metamorphosis was completed; and now I would like to see another metamorphosis take place in the opposite direction. Suppose my bull's head is thrown on the scrap heap. Perhaps some day a fellow will come along and say: 'Why there's something that would come in very handy for the handlebars of my bicycle...' and so a double metamorphosis would have been achieved.[10]

Remembrance of former function and value (bicycles and minotaurs); shifting context; an attitude which encourages the composite; an exploitation and re-cycling of meaning (has there ever been enough to go around?); desuetude of function with corresponding agglomeration of reference; memory; anticipation; the connectedness of memory and wit; the integrity of wit: this is a laundry list of reactions to Picasso's proposition; and, since it is a proposition evidently addressed to people, it is in terms such as these, in terms of pleasures remembered and desired, of a dialectic between past and future, of an impacting of iconographic content, of a temporal as well as a spatial collision, that resuming an earlier argument, one might proceed to specify an ideal city of the mind.

With Picasso's image one asks: what is false and what is true, what

Picasso: Still life with chair caning,
1911-12

is antique and what is 'of today'; and it is because of an inability to make
half way adequate reply to this pleasing difficulty that one, finally, is
obliged to identify the problem of composite presence in terms of *collage*.

Collage and the architect's conscience, collage as technique and
collage as state of mind: Lévi-Strauss tells us that 'the intermittent
fashion for 'collages', originating when craftsmanship was dying, could
not...be anything but the transposition of 'bricolage' into the realms of
contemplation'[11] and, if the twentieth century architect has been the
reverse of willing to think of himself as a 'bricoleur' it is in this context
that one must also place his frigidity in relation to major twentieth
century discovery. Collage has seemed to be lacking in sincerity, to
represent a corruption of moral principles, an adulteration. One thinks
of Picasso's *Still life with chair caning* of 1911-12, his first collage, and
begins to understand why.

In analysing this, Alfred Barr speaks of:

...the section of chair caning which is neither real nor painted but is
actually a piece of oil cloth facsimile pasted on the canvas and then partly
painted over. Here in one picture Picasso juggles reality and abstraction
in two media and at four different levels or ratios...[And] if we stop to
think which is the most 'real' we find ourselves moving from aesthetic to
metaphysical contemplation. For what seems most real is most false and
what seems most remote from everyday reality is perhaps the most real
since it is *least an imitation*.[12]

And the oil cloth facsimile of chair caning, an *objet trouvé* snatched

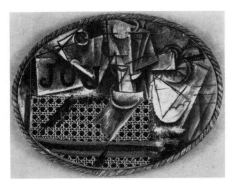

top
Le Corbusier: Paris, Ozenfant studio,
1922

below
Picasso: Still life with chair caning,
1911-12

from the underworld of 'low' culture and catapulted into the super-world of 'high' art, might illustrate the architect's dilemma. Collage is simultaneously innocent and devious.

Indeed among architects only that great straddler Le Corbusier, sometimes hedgehog, sometimes fox, has displayed any sympathy towards this kind of thing. His buildings, though not his city plans, are loaded with the results of a process which might be considered more or less equivalent to that of collage. Objects and episodes are obtrusively imported and, while they retain the overtones of their source and origin, they gain also a wholly new impact from their changed context. In, for instance, the Ozenfant studio one is confronted with a mass of allusions and references which it would seem are all basically brought together by collage means.

Disparate objects held together by various means, 'physical, optical, psychological,' 'the oil cloth with its sharp focussed facsimile detail and its surface apparently so rough yet actually so smooth...partly absorbed into both the painted surface and the painted forms by letting both overlap it.'[13] With very slight modifications (for oil cloth caning substitute fake industrial glazing, for painted surface substitute wall, etc.) Alfred Barr's observations could be directly carried over into interpreta-

above
Le Corbusier: Marseilles, Unité
d'Habitation, 1946, roofscape

above left
Le Corbusier: Paris, terrace of the
De Beistegui penthouse, 1930-1

centre
Le Corbusier: house at Bordeaux-
Pessac, 1925, interior

below
Le Corbusier: Nestlé exhibition
pavilion, 1928

Lubetkin and Tecton: London, Highpoint 2, 1938, view of porte-cochère

tion of the Ozenfant studio. And further illustrations of Le Corbusier as collagiste cannot be hard to find: the too obvious De Beistegui penthouse, the roofscapes—ships and mountains—of Poissy and Marseilles, random rubble at the Porte Molitor and the Pavillon Suisse, an interior from Bordeaux-Pessac and, particularly, the Nestlé exhibition pavilion of 1928.

But, of course, beyond Le Corbusier the evidences of this state of mind are sparse and have been scarcely well received. One thinks of Lubetkin at Highpoint II with his Erectheion caryatids and pretended imitations of the house painter imitating wood; one thinks of Moretti at the Casa del Girasole—simulated antique fragments in the *piano rustico*; and one thinks of Albini at the Palazzo Rosso, also one may think of Charles Moore. The list is not extensive but its briefness makes admirable testimony. It is a commentary upon exclusiveness. For collage, often a method of paying attention to the left-overs of the world, of preserving their integrity and equipping them with dignity, of compounding matter of factness and cerebrality, as a convention and a breach of convention, necessarily operates unexpectedly. A rough method, 'a kind of *discordia concors*; a combination of dissimilar images, or discovery of occult

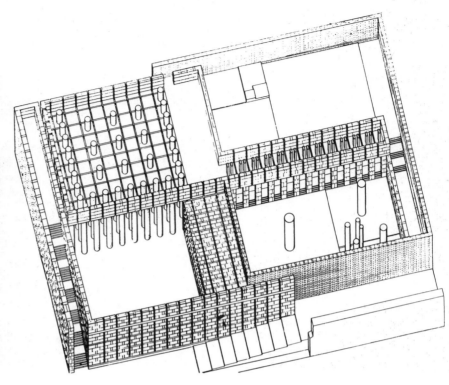

above
Luigi Moretti: Rome, Casa del Girasole, detail

above right
Guiseppe Terragni: Rome, project for Danteum, 1938. Terragni's Danteum may also be regarded as an influential specimen of collage. The crystal columns of its interior presumably relate to the location of Terragni's early military service in the Palazzo del Giardino in Parma. In this building Bertoia's frescoes of the Sala del Bacio (1566-71) seem to prefigure Terragni's idea.

resemblances in things apparently unlike', Samuel Johnson's remarks upon the poetry of John Donne,[14] which could also be remarks upon Stravinsky, Eliot, Joyce, upon much of the programme of Synthetic Cubism, are indicative of the absolute reliance of collage upon a juggling of norms and recollections, upon a backward look which, for those who think of history and the future as exponential progression towards ever more perfect simplicity, can only prompt the judgement that collage, for all its psychological virtuosity (Anna Livia, all alluvial), is a wilfully interjected impediment to the strict route of evolution.

Such one knows to be the judgement of the architect's tradition of modernity: the times are far too serious for play, the course is plotted, the promptings of destiny not to be denied.[15] One may expand the objections at will; but one must also construct the counter argument which presupposes seriousness, hopes for amelioration, but which still maintains a sceptical distance from big visions of social deliverance. And the argument is obviously that between two conceptions of time. On the one hand time becomes the metronome of progress, its serial aspects are given cumulative and dynamic presence; while, on the other, though sequence and chronology are recognized for the facts which they are, time, deprived of some of its linear imperatives, is allowed to rearrange itself according to experiential schemata. In terms of the one argument the commission of anachronism is the ultimate of all possible sins. In terms of the other the conception of date is of minor consequence. Marinetti's:

When lives have to be sacrificed we are not saddened if before our minds shines the magnificent harvest of a superior life which will arise from their deaths... We are on the extreme promontory of the centuries! What is the use of looking behind... we are already living in the absolute, since we have already created eternal omnipresent speed. We sing of great crowds agitated by work; the multi-coloured and polyphonic surf of revolution.

and his later:

The victory of Vittorio Veneto and the coming to power of Fascism constitute the realisation of the minimal Futurist programme... Futurism is strictly artistic and ideological... Prophets and forerunners of the great Italy of today, we Futurists are happy to salute in our not yet forty year old prime minister a marvellous Futurist temperament.[16]

might be a *reductio ad absurdum* of the one argument; and Picasso's:

To me there is no past and no future in art... The several manners which I have used in my art must not be considered as an evolution or as steps towards an unknown ideal of painting... All I have ever made was made for the present and with the hope that it will always remain in the present.[17]

could be allowed to represent an extreme statement of the other. In theological terms the one argument is eschatological, the other incarnational; but, while they may both of them be necessary, the cooler and more comprehensive nature of the second argument might still excite attention. *The second argument might include the first but the reverse can never be true*; and, with so much said, we might now re-approach collage as a serious instrument.

Presented with Marinetti's chronolatry and Picasso's a-temporality; presented with Popper's critique of historicism (which is also Futurism/futurism); presented with the difficulties of both utopia and tradition, with the problems of both violence and atrophy; presented with alleged libertarian impulse and alleged need for the security of order; presented with the sectarian tightness of the architect's ethical corset and with more reasonable visions of catholicity; presented with contraction and expansion; we ask what other resolution of social problems is possible outside the, admitted, limitations of collage. Limitations which should be obvious enough; but limitations which still prescribe and assure an open territory.

It is suggested that a collage approach, an approach in which objects are conscripted or seduced from out of their context, is—at the present day—the only way of dealing with the ultimate problems of, either or both, utopia and tradition; and the provenance of the architectural objects introduced into the social collage need not be of great consequence. It relates to taste and conviction. The objects can be aristocratic or they can be 'folkish', academic or popular. Whether they originate in Pergamum or Dahomey, in Detroit or Dubrovnik, whether their implications are of the twentieth or the fifteenth century, is no great matter. Societies and persons assemble themselves according to their own interpretations of absolute reference and traditional value; and, up to a point, collage accommodates both hybrid display and the requirements of self-determination.

But up to a point: for if the city of collage may be more hospitable than the city of modern architecture, it cannot more than any human institution pretend to be *completely* hospitable. The ideally open city, like the ideally open society, is just as much a figment of the imagination as its opposite. The open and the closed society, either envisaged as practical possibilities, are both of them the caricatures of contrary ideals; and it is to the realms of caricature that one should choose to relegate all extreme fantasies of both emancipation and control. The arguments of Popper and Habermas may be conceded; the desideratum of the open society and the emancipatory interest is evident; the need for the reconstruction of an operative critical theory after its long negation by scientism, historicism, psychologism should be equally so; but one may still be concerned, in this Popperian area, with an imbalance comparable to that in his critiques of tradition and utopia. This can seem to be a too exclusive focus upon concrete evils and a corresponding reluctance to attempt any construction of abstract goods. Concrete evils are identifiable–there can be consensus about them, but abstract goods (apart from the highly abstract emancipatory interest) remain a difficult commodity–they evade agreement; and therefore, while the criticist pursuit and eradication of concrete evil becomes libertarian, all attempts to stipulate abstract good–because of their inevitable foundation in dogma–begin to be envisaged as coercive.

So it is with the problems of dogma (hot dogma, cool dogma, mere dogma), all abundantly segregated by Popper, that the issue of ideal type again emerges. The Popperian social philosophy is an affair of attack and *détente*–of attack upon conditions and ideas not making for *détente*; and it is, up to a point, sympathetic. But this intellectual position which simultaneously envisages the existence of heavy industry and Wall Street (as traditions to be criticized) and then also postulates the existence of an ideal theatre of argument (a Rousseau version of the Swiss canton with its organic *Tagesatzung?*) may also inspire scepticism.

The Rousseau version of the Swiss canton (which had very little use for Rousseau), the comparable New England town meeting (white paint and witch hunt?), the eighteenth century House of Commons, the ideal academic faculty meeting (and what to say about that?): undoubtedly these–along with miscellaneous soviets, kibbutzim and other references to tribal society–belong to the few theatres of logical and equal discourse so far projected or erected. But, if there should obviously be more of them, then, while one speculates about their architecture, one

is also compelled to ask whether these are simply traditional constructs. Which is first to intrude the ideal dimension of these various theatres; and which is then to ask whether specific traditions (awaiting criticism) are in any way conceivable without that great body of anthropological tradition involving magic, ritual and the centrality of ideal type, and presuming utopia as an incipient presence.

In other words, conceding the criticist argument and conceding the categorical imperative of emancipation, we return to the problems of scaffold and exhibit, the problems of the exhibit/demonstration/critical act which will remain invisible (and unprovoked) so long as not supported by a far from auxiliary apparatus of isolation, framing and light. For, just as utopia has traditionally been a mandala, a device for concentrating and protecting ideas, so—and equally—tradition has never been without its utopian component. 'This is a government of laws not men', an important, a dogmatic and a highly American statement which is both absurd and eminently comprehensible—absurd in its utopian and classical protestation, comprehensible (in despite of 'people') in its appeal to a magical efficacy which, occasionally, may even serve pragmatic purpose.

And it is the notion of the law, the neutral background which illustrates and stimulates the particular ('the law entered that the offence might abound'[18]), the notion of the law, inherently a matter of precedent but also conceiving itself to be an ideal formulation, either given in nature or imposed upon it by divine will—in any case magically sanctioned and not man made, it is the constitution of this sometimes incredible but always necessary fiction, which equips itself with both empirical and ideal, traditional and utopian overtones, which operates with a double ethic, which evolves in history but which insists on platonic reference, it is this very public institution which must now be gainfully employed in commentary upon the scaffold-exhibit relationship.

Renato Poggioli speaks of 'the failure of the attempt to realize a modern marvelous (almost always scientific in content, almost exclusively urban in ambiance)';[19] and, in the concept of 'modern marvelous',

The mandala as *axis mundi*

we can easily recognize the presence of those visions of a permanently limpid social order by which the modern city was to be animated and sustained, visions of a social order that was to derive and maintain its value by means of a wholly accurate and automatically self-renewing perception of fact, a perception at once scientific and poetic, which could only assign to fact the role of miracle. This is the type of *miracle scaffold of the measurable* which presents itself as benign (a government of neither laws *nor* men), as a cathedral of popular faith in the scientific imagination (excluding the need for both imagination and faith), as an edifice where all contingencies have been taken care of (where questions no more remain). But it is also the type of miracle-marvel, the icon whose presence speaks for itself, which, presuming its legality, eradicates the requirements of both judgement and debate, which can neither accept nor be accepted by any degree of reasonable scepticism, and which is infinitely more dreadful than any legal construct. Certainly the government of neither laws nor men: at this stage Hannah Ahrendt's 'most tyrannical government of all...the government of nobody, the total-itarianism of technique'[20] can only enter the picture.

The overt proclamation of liberty and the surreptitious insistence that liberty (founded in fact) must exist apart from human volition, the determination to leave unconsidered such structures of mediation as are obviously man made ('I do not like the police'),[21] the nihilistic gesture which is rooted in misunderstood, and misinterpreted, abundance: it is in connection with all this that we have proposed a contemplation of the elementary and enlivening duplicities of law, 'natural' and traditional, of that conflict between an ethical and a 'scientific' ideal which, so long as maintained, at least facilitates interpretation.

But all of this, proposing an order of release through the media of both utopia and tradition, through the city as museum, through collage as both exhibit and scaffold, through the dubieties and duplicities of law, through the precariousness of fact and the eel-like slipperiness of meaning, through the complete absence of simple certainty, is also to propose a situation (which may seem utopian) in which the demands of activist utopia have receded, in which the time bomb of historical deter-minism is at last defused, in which the requirements of composite time have become finally established, and in which that strange idea, the eternal present, becomes effectively reinstated alongside its equally strange competitors.

The open field and the closed field: we have already suggested the value of the one as a political necessity, of the other as an instrument of negotiation, identity, perception; but, if the conceptual functions of both of them should not require to be emphasized, it might still be noticed that the predicament of the open spatial field and the closed temporal field must, of necessity, be as absurd as that of its opposite. It was the lavish perspectives of cultural time, the historical depths and profund-ities of Europe (or wherever else culture was presumed to be located) as against the exotic insignificance of 'the rest', which most furnished the architecture of previous ages; and it has been the opposite condition which has distinguished that of our own day—a willingness to abolish almost all the taboos of physical distance, the barriers of space, and then, alongside this, a corresponding determination to erect the most relentless of temporal frontiers. One thinks of that chronological iron curtain which, in the minds of the devout, quarantines modern architecture from all the infections of free-wheeling temporal association; but, while we recognize its former justification (identity, incubation, the hot house), the reasons for artificially maintaining such a temperature of enthusiasm can now only begin to seem very remote.

For when one recognizes that restriction of free trade, whether in space or time, cannot, for ever, be profitably sustained, that without free trade the diet becomes restricted and provincialized, the survival of the imagination endangered, and that, ultimately, there must ensue some kind of insurrection of the senses, this is only to identify one aspect of the situation which may be conceived. Like the open society as a fact, the ideal of unrestricted free trade must be a chimera. We are apt to believe that the global village will only breed global village idiots; and it is in the light of this supposition that the ideal Swiss canton of the mind, trafficked but isolated, and the New England village of the picture postcard, closed but open to all the imports of mercantile venture, begin again to clamour for attention. For an acceptance of free trade need not require complete dependence upon it and the benefits of free trade are not entirely obliged to lead to a rampage of the libido.

In issues such as these the ideal Swiss canton of the mind and the New England community of the picture postcard are reputed to have always maintained a stubborn and calculated balance of identity and advantage. That is: to survive they could only present two faces; and, if to the world they became exhibit, for themselves they could only remain scaffold. Which, because it is a qualification that *must* be laid upon the idea of free trade, could, before conclusion, allow occasion to recall Lévi-Strauss's precarious 'balance between structure and event, necessity and contingency, the internal and the external...'

Now a collage technique, by intention if not by definition, insists upon the centrality of just such a balancing act. A balancing act? But:

Wit, you know, is the unexpected copulation of ideas, the discovery of some occult relation between images in appearance remote from each other; and an effusion of wit, therefore, presupposes an accumulation of knowledge; a memory stored with notions, which the imagination may cull out to compose new assemblages. Whatever may be the native vigour of the mind, she can never form many combinations from few ideas, as many changes can never be rung upon a few bells. Accident may indeed sometimes produce a lucky parallel or a striking contrast; but these gifts of chance are not frequent, and he that has nothing of his own, and yet condemns himself to needless expenses must live upon loans or theft.[22]

Samuel Johnson, again, provides a far better definition of something very like collage than any we are capable of producing; and surely some such state of mind should inform all approaches to both utopia and tradition.

We think again of Hadrian. We think of the 'private' and diverse scene at Tivoli. At the same time we think of the Mausoleum (Castel Sant'Angelo) and the Pantheon in their metropolitan locations. And particularly we think of the Pantheon, of its oculus. Which may lead one to contemplate the publicity of necessarily singular intention (keeper of Empire) and the privacy of elaborate personal interests—a situation which is not at all like that of *ville radieuse* versus the Villa Stein at Garches.

Habitually utopia, whether platonic or Marxian, has been conceived of as *axis mundi* or as *axis istoriae*; but, if in this way it has operated like all totemic, traditionalist and uncriticized aggregations of ideas, if its existence has been poetically necessary and politically deplorable, then this is only to assert the idea that a collage technique, by accommodating a whole range of *axes mundi* (all of them vest pocket utopias—Swiss canton, New England village, Dome of the Rock, Place Vendome, Campidoglio, etc., might be a means of permitting us the enjoyment of utopian poetics without our being obliged to suffer the embarrassment of utopian politics. Which is to say that, because collage is a method deriving its virtue from its irony, because it seems to be a technique for using things and simultaneously disbelieving in them, it is also a strategy which can allow utopia to be dealt with as image, to be dealt with in *fragments* without our having to accept it *in toto*, which is further to suggest that collage could even be a strategy which, by supporting the utopian illusion of changelessness and finality, might even fuel a reality of change, motion, action and history.

I understand; you speak of that city of which we are the founders, and which exists in idea only for I do not think there is such an one anywhere on earth.

In heaven, I replied, there is laid up a pattern of such a city, and he who desires may behold this, and beholding, govern himself accordingly. But whether there really is or ever will be such an one is of no importance to him; for he will act according to the laws of that city and of no other.

PLATO, *Republic*, Book IX (Jowett trans.)

Michelangelo: Rome, paving of the
Piazza del Campidoglio as completed in
1940

Excursus

We append an abridged list of stimulants, a-temporal and necessarily transcultural, as possible *objets trouvés* in the urbanistic collage.

Memorable streets

First of all certain *memorable streets*: from Edinburgh the one sided Princes Street; from New York its grown up equivalent, the great wall of Fifth Avenue along Central Park with the North British hotel become the Plaza; from Paris, as a type of simplified Uffizi, the Rue des Colonnes; from Karlsruhe Friedrich Weinbrenner's project for the Langen Strasse; from old Berlin the amassed spectacle of the Unter den Linden and the Lustgarten; from unbuilt Berlin Van Eesteren's project of 1925 for part of the same sequence; from Genoa the Strada Nuova.

above
New York, Fifth Avenue along Central Park

below
Edinburgh, Princes Street

Friedrich Weinbrenner:
Karlsruhe, project for Langen-
(Kaiser-) strasse, 1808

Paris, rue des Colonnes, 1791

Berlin, Unter den Linden, 1842

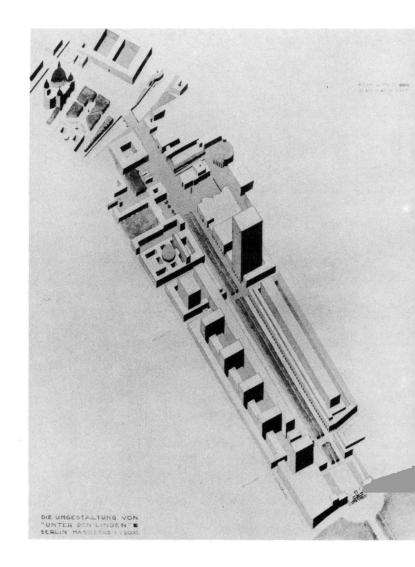

Cor Van Eesteren: Berlin,
project for Unter den Linden,
1925

Above
Genoa, Strada Nuova, air view

Below
Genoa, Strada Nuova, plan

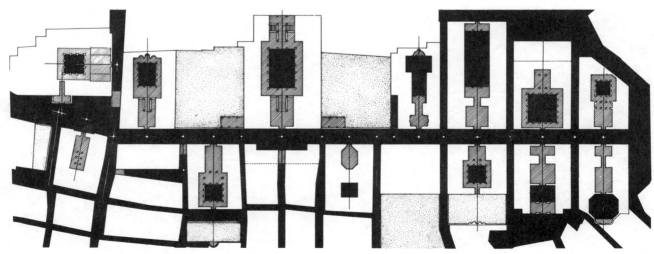

Stabilizers

Then, moving from linear progression to centric emphasis, a number of
magically useless *stabilizers*, points or navels which essentially exhibit
a coherent geometry. Accompanied by buildings this category might
include: from Vigevano its piazza; from Paris the Place des Vosges; from
Vittoria the Plaza Mayor; and, entirely detached from any immediate
closure: from Rome the Mausoleum of Augustus as it presented itself
in the seventeenth century; from Padua the Prato della Valle; from
Valsanzibio the rabbit island.

below
Paris, Place des Vosges (Place Royale)

right
Vigevano, Piazza Ducale

right below
Vittoria, Plaza Mayor

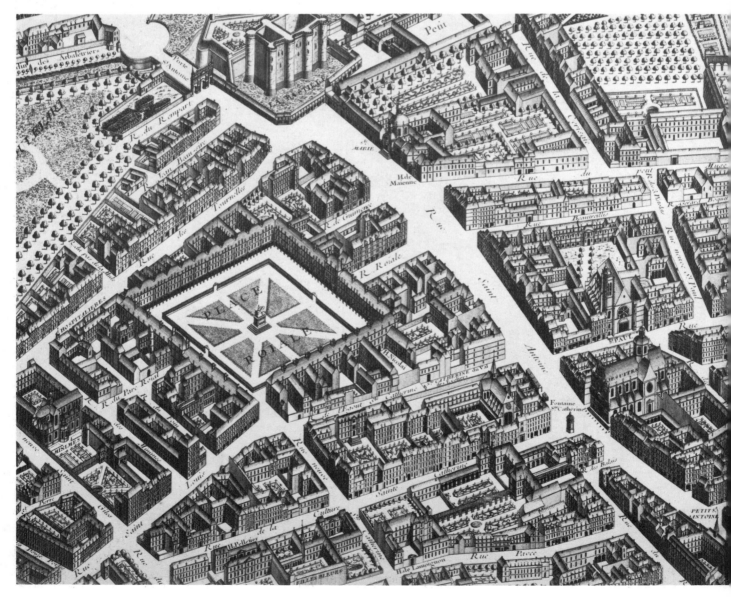

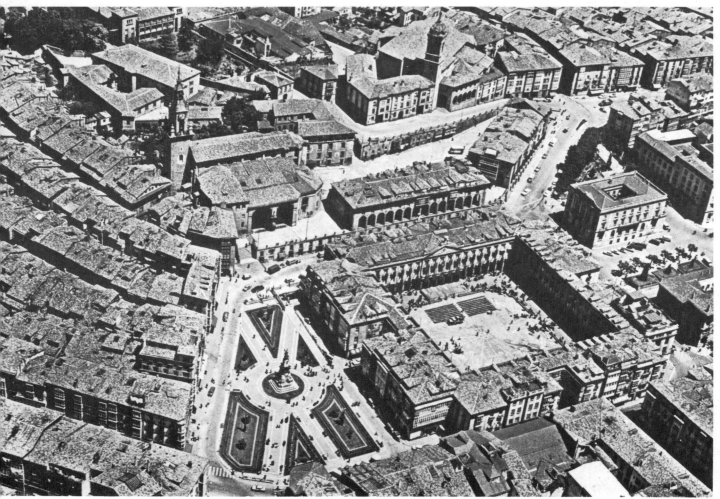

above
Padua, Prato della Valle

right
Rome, Mausoleum of Augustus

right below
Valsanzibio, Villa Barbarigo,
the Rabbit Island

Potentially interminable set pieces

Next a group of *potentially interminable set pieces* among which, from ancient Rome, the relentlessly extended Porticus Aemilia might be cited; but, if this particular performance might provide too literal an illustration of a repetitive exercise which distends the eye, then one may associate with it: from Athens the Stoa of Attalos; from Vicenza its partner the Palazzo Chiericati; from Venice the Procuratie Vecchie; from Paris the Grande Galerie of the Louvre; and, with slightly different inflections: from unbuilt Hamburg, Heinrich De Fries's project for the Exportmesse and, from Regent's Park in London, the theatrical backdrop of Chester Terrace.

below
Rome, the Porticus Aemilia

right above
Athens, Stoa of Attalos

right below
Vicenza, Palazzo Chiericati

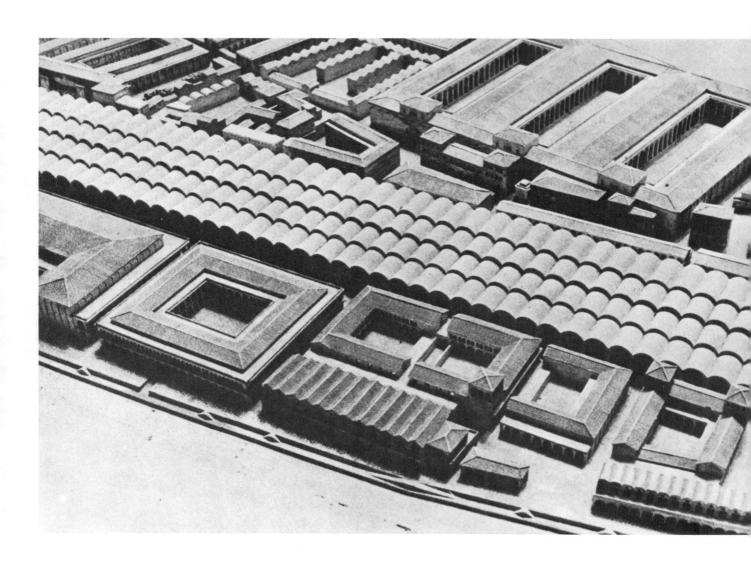

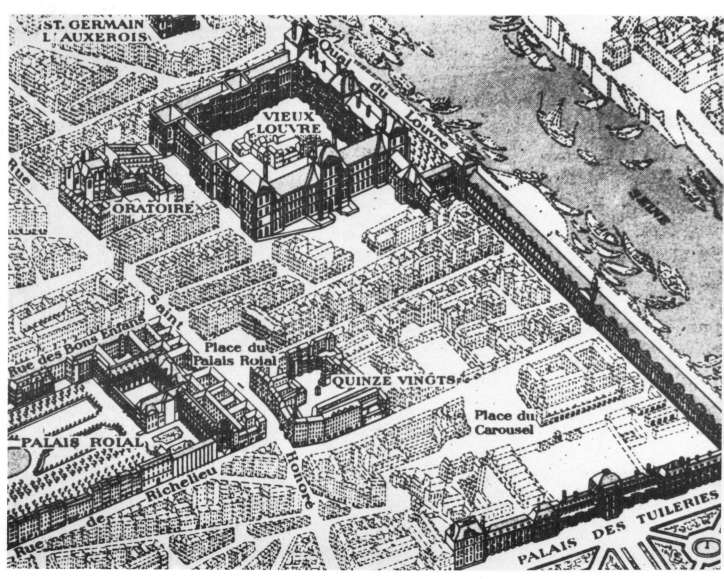

left above
London, Chester Terrace

left below
Paris, Louvre and Tuileries

above
Heinrich de Fries: Hamburg, project
for the Exportmesse, 1925

below
Venice, Procuratie Vecchie

Splendid public terraces

Among further items a number of *splendid public terraces*, commanding sometimes landscape sometimes water: from Rome the Pincio; from Florence the Piazzale Michelangelo; again from Vicenza the platform of the Monte Berico—all of them destinations and to be compared with the type of terrace promenade which might include: from vanished London Robert Adam's Adelphi; from Algiers the astonishing extravaganza, part Durand part Piranesi of the waterfront; which, from unbuilt Baden-Baden, might be prefaced by the ramping and terraced suburbia of Max Laeuger's project for the Friedrichspark.

above
Rome, Pincio
below
Vicenza, Piazzale Monte Berico
right
Florence, Piazzale Michelangelo

above
London, Adelphi Terrace

below
Algiers, the waterfront

right
Max Laeuger: Baden-Baden, project for the Friedrichspark Siedlung, 1926

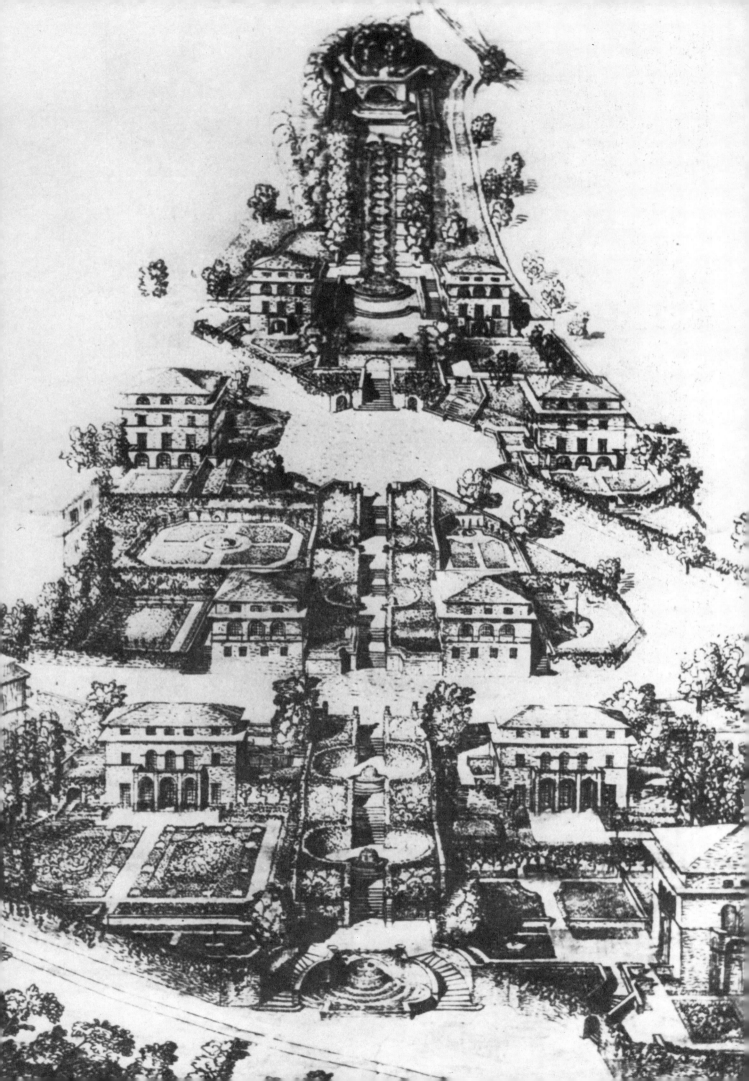

Ambiguous and composite buildings

Next a series of *ambiguous and composite buildings*, urban mega-structures if need be, all of them far from 'modern' but all of them engaging circumstance and rising above it: from Vienna the Hofburg; from Munich the Residenz; from a Dresden that is no longer, the group of bridge, Bruhlscheterrasse, schloss

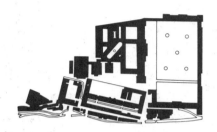

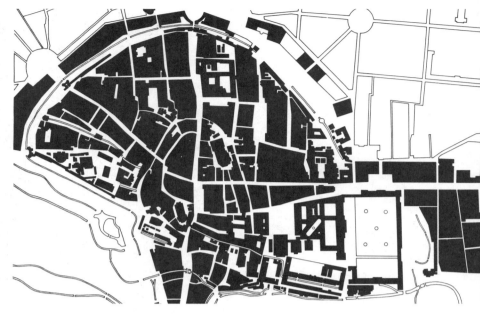

Munich, Residenz, figure-ground plan

and Zwinger. To which might be added: the triangular chateau of Compiègne in its relationship to town and park; the relation of town to park at Franzesbad; the palace-city relationship at Jaipur; comparable conditions at Ispahan;

and possibly, as an Indian version of the Villa Adriana, the amazing distributions at Fatephur Sikri. These are, all of them, regular/irregular and more than a little wild. They, all of them, oscillate (and in different parts) between a passive and an active

Dresden, Zwinger, figure-ground plan

behaviour. They, all of them, both quietly collaborate and strenuously assert. They, all of them, are occasionally ideal. But, above all, this series is highly accessible to a present sensibility and, of its nature, is capable of almost every local accommodation.

Vienna, Hofburg, figure-ground plan

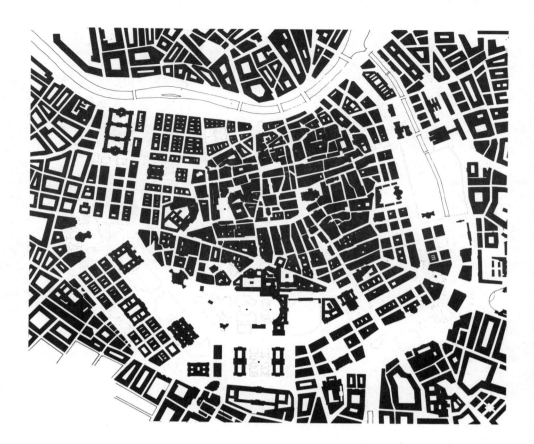

Compiègne, town and chateau, figure-ground plan

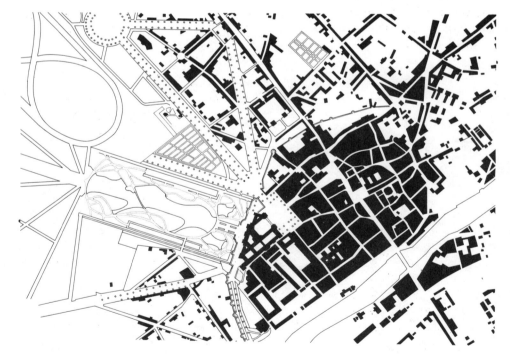

Jaipur, palace, figure-ground plan

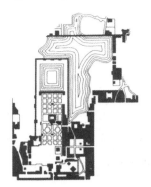

Ispahan, plan

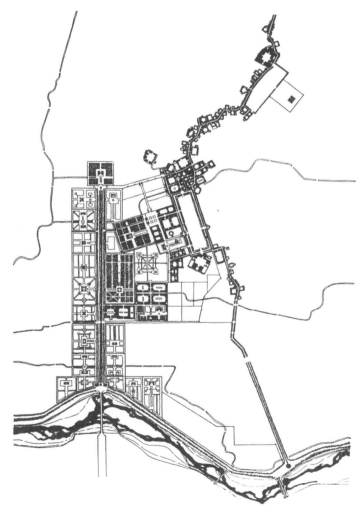

Fatephur Sikri, figure-ground plan

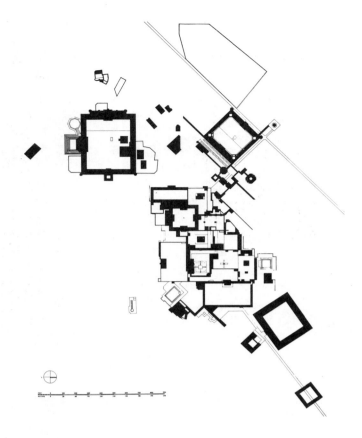

Franzensbad, figure-ground plan

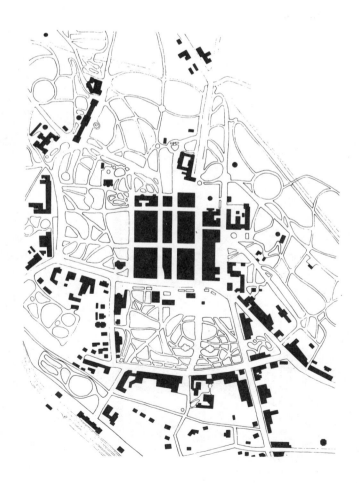

Nostalgia-producing instruments

Finally, a quantity of *nostalgia producing instruments* which may be 'scientific' and of the future, 'romantic' and of the past, or which, in different ways, may be simply elegant vernacular or Pop. And, in this context, one thinks of offshore oil rigs, the pyramid of Caius Cestius, rocket launching and indoor climates at Cape Canaveral, the Vignola (?) *tempietto* at Bomarzo, old Roman tombs, small town America, a Vauban fort, and the Las Vegas or any other strip so adored by the Venturis.

1 Las Vegas, The Strip

2 Offshore oil rig

3 Rome, pyramid of Caius Cestius

4 Galena, Illinois

5 Cape Canaveral, Florida

6 Cape Canaveral

7 Bomarzo, garden temple

8 fortifications of Montlouis

9 fortifications of Briançon

7

8

9

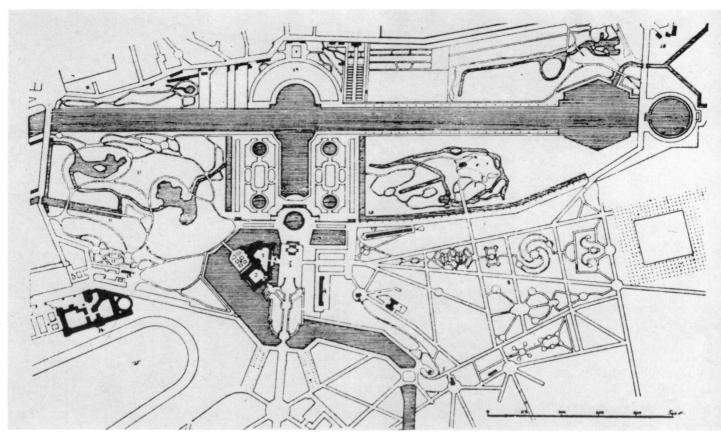

above Chantilly, plan of chateau and park   *below* Stowe, the Bridgeman garden plan

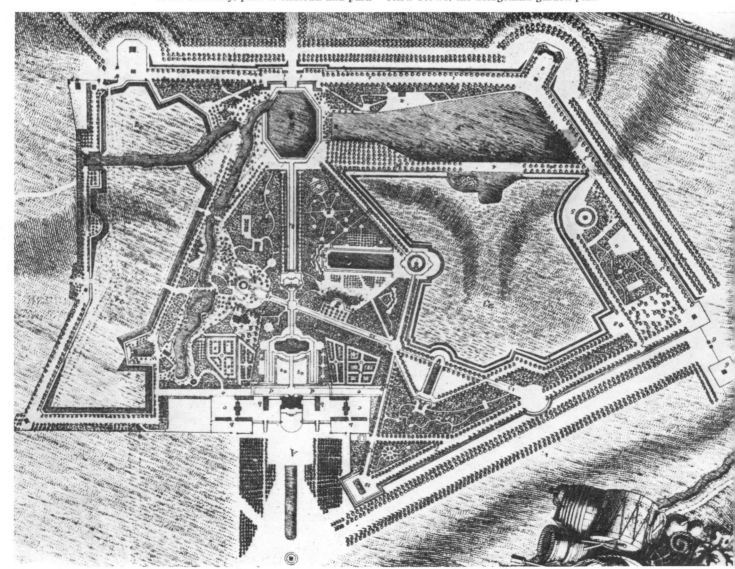

The garden

But all of these observations/
discriminations which primarily
record 'events' are to be understood
as quasi-absorbed in some prevalent
'structure', matrix, or fabric which
might be regular or irregular and,
in its spread, either horizontal or
vertical. Regular and irregular
instances of horizontal matrices
should scarcely require calling out:
the texture of Manhattan and the
texture of Boston; the pattern of
Turin and the more random pattern
of Siena; and, in the area of semi-
solid structures, the highly perforated
grid of Savannah and the more
casual agglomerations of Oxford–
Cambridge; and instances of
prevailing vertical matrices should be
no less obvious: the urban wallpaper
of Venice, of the Rue de Rivoli, or of
Regent's Park; the gabled three-bay
façades of Amsterdam; the colossal,
hip-roofed, pretensions of Genoa; in
the upper east side of Manhattan
that strange combination of palatial
Genoa in the avenues and
domesticated Amsterdam in the

streets; and, finally, the American
street of the nineteenth century with
the uniformity of its white painted
houses and their continuous framing
in an apparatus of small lawns and a
shadowing lattice of huge elm
trees.

And the American nineteenth
century street, a matter of intricate
white figures sustained by an all
pervasive grid of green, an unlikely
culmination of so much that was
implicit in the programme of
Romantic Classicism, a street which
can, sometimes, be almost unbearably
idyllic and arcadian, a species of
garden though by no means a species
of garden city, this street which is so
little advertised and so little recorded
may now serve as a fulcrum for a
further interjection of stimulants.

The garden as a criticism of the
city and hence as a model city. This
is a theme which has already been
introduced and which should
deserve attention. So fragments of
Washington, D.C. provide almost a
literal reproduction of the gardens

and park of Versailles; Second
Empire Paris is something of a built
replica of a collection of gardens in
the style of Le Nôtre; and the
American romantic suburb (Turtle
Creek, Grosse Pointe Farms) is
evidently affiliated to such English
gardens as Stourhead and the later
conditions of Stowe, but, such too
obvious transpositions apart, the
potential of the garden, what should
be its suggestiveness for the
'planner' or the 'designer' of cities,
continues to be very little noticed.

Therefore, simply to observe that,
if the garden may offer the presence
of a constructed situation independent
of the necessity of any buildings,
then gardens *may* be useful; and we
think not so much of the
acknowledged set pieces, not so
much of Vaux-le-Vicomte as
Chantilly, not so much of Versailles
as of the impacted and Hadrianic
disarray represented by Bridgeman's

below
chateau of Verneuil

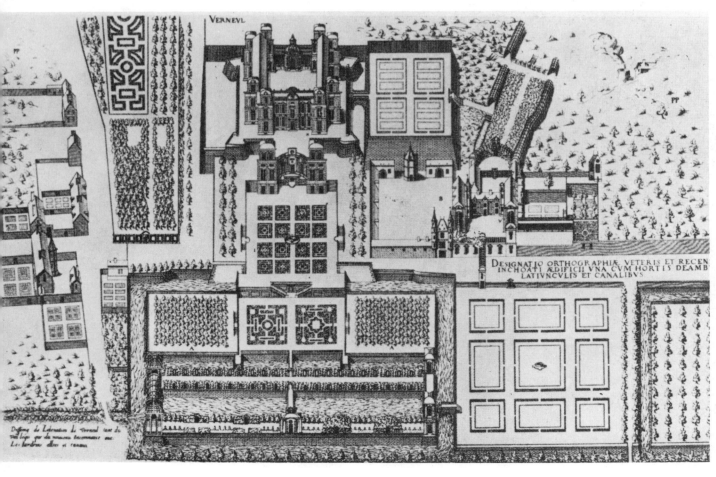

Stowe. The influence of the too
platonic, too Cartesian and too
arcadian garden has, so far,
dominated; and, against these, we
would prefer to admire certain
conditions of randomness and order–
mostly French.

Thus; after Chantilly which, with
the grandeur of its plateau and the
casual arrogance of its axis, with its
implications of Descartes and its
shades of Shaftesbury, with the
exaggerated precision of its masonry
and its careless throwaways, is
surely the most comprehensive of
gardens (and the most promising of
cities); and, after the Anglo-French
of Bridgeman's Stowe (just how much
can you agitate a bland terrain?) we
would cite: Verneuil (which, as
presented by Du Cerceau, excited Le
Corbusier) and then a variety of
unacknowledged and sometimes
provincial pieces.

above
chateau of the Bishops of Langres
below
chateau of Colbert de Villacerf

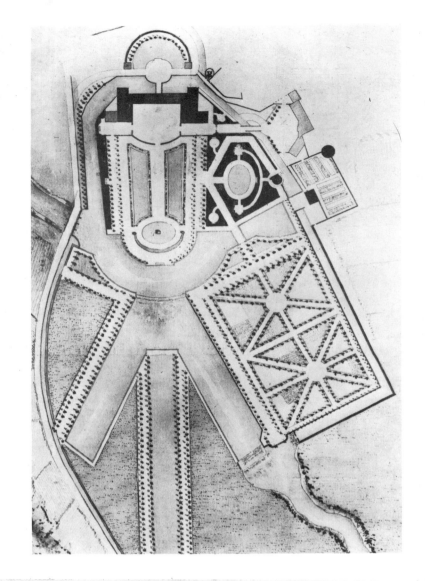

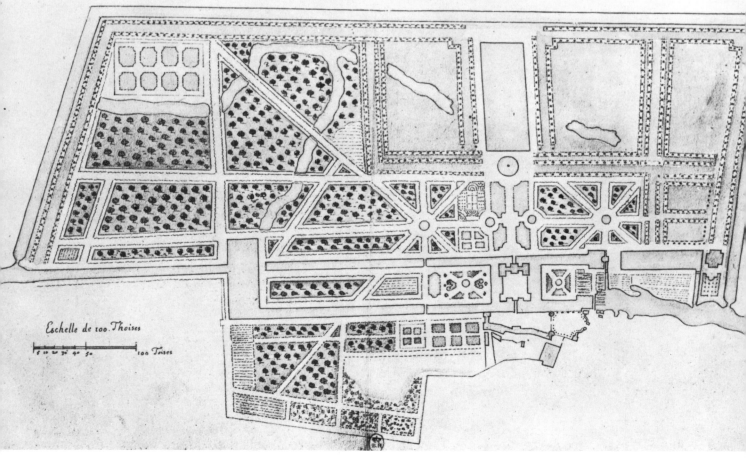

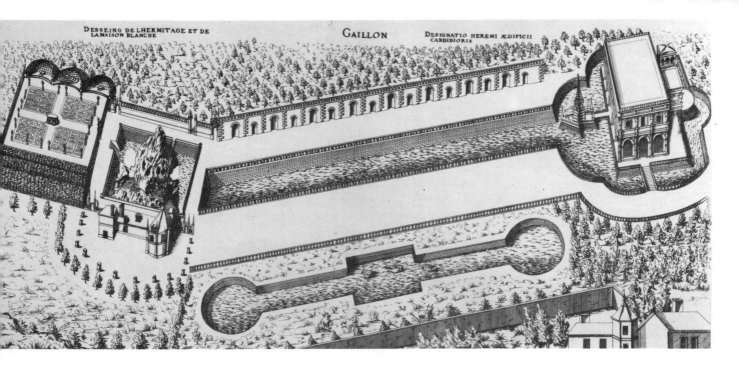

hateau of Gaillon

aris, Parc Monceau

Accordingly, from Stein's *Jardins de France* we extract two rather primitive items: the chateau of Colbert de Villacerf and the not entirely equivalent chateau of the Bishops of Langres. The scene of the Bishops of Langres presents an obviously old house, probably refaced, but equipped with appropriate garden and gesture; but Colbert de Villacerf, with its almost Chinese grid of canals and counter water pieces, might also present one of the most important of references. And, to these, we would wish merely to annex the highly delicate Parc Monceau which, as a Le Nôtre style distribution violated by lyrical imperatives, speaks for itself; and, finally, a highly assertive, slightly frenzied episode which Du Cerceau records as at Gaillon.

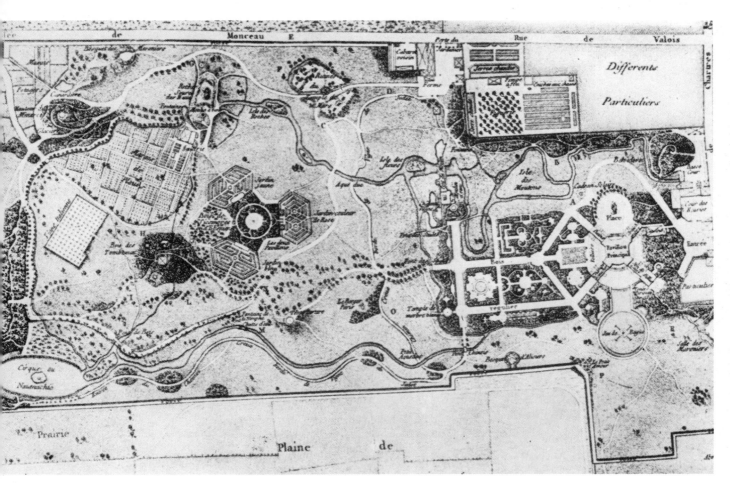

Commentary

'These fragments I have shored against my ruins': T.S. Eliot's use of verbal *objets trouvés* in *The Waste Land* could leap to mind; but Canaletto's view of an imaginary Rialto equipped with a whole array of Palladian buildings, when it is compared with the reality of the site, might be allowed further to imply some of the arguments of *Collage City*. With the Palazzo dei Camerlenghi replaced by the Basilica, the Fondaco dei Tedeschi superseded by the Palazzo Chiericati, and with a reminiscence of the Casa Civena lurking in the background, the observer is subjected to a double shock of recognition. Is this an idealized Venice, or is it a Vicenza which might have been? The question must always remain open; and William Marlow's view of St. Paul's in a Venetian setting inevitably contributes to the same theatre of speculation. But illustrations of the transferability of buildings abound; and, at a less prosaic level, Nicolas Poussin's architectural backgrounds

Poussin: Landscape with the ashes of
Phocion collected by his widow

offer comparable cities of composite
presence. Poussin's manipulation of
his architectural *objets à réaction
poétique* is, of course, infinitely more
impeccable and evocative than
anything of which Canaletto and
Marlow were capable. The first
titillate the informed traveller, the
second move the heart; and, in
Poussin's imaginary cities everything
becomes classically condensed. In,
for instance, the Knowsley *Phocion*
the city of Megara, an Italian village
of far more than usual quality, is
dominated by an accurate replica
(again from Palladio) of the temple at
Trevi; while in the Louvre's *Christ*

Healing the Blind Men, the village of
Nazareth presents a Romano-Venetic
anthology comprising a close version
of Palladio's unbuilt Villa Garzadore,
an early Christian basilica which is
not quite a facsimile of anything,
and another house of which the
appearance suggests that it ought to
have been built by Vincenzo
Scamozzi.

A protracted backward look could
involve many more instances of
just this style of amalgamation (for
instance, Jan Van Eyck's
simultaneously Romanesque and
Gothic backgrounds for the Ghent
Adoration of the Lamb); but the

Poussin: Christ healing the blind men

issue, surely, does not require to be
pursued. For, fundamentally, the city
of composite presence is too
pervasive an idea ever to become
outdated; and one must, therefore,
still ask why the subjective, synthetic
procedures which characterize it have
for so long been conceived of as
reprehensible. Thus, for all its
coercions, the utopian city of the
abstractive intellect still remains
respectable, while the far more
benevolent metropolis of loosely
organized sympathies and enthusiasms
continues to appear illegitimate. But,
if utopia is a necessary idea, no less
and no more important should be

that other city of the mind which the
vedute fantastiche of Canaletto and the
collaged backgrounds of Poussin
both represent and prefigure.
Utopia as metaphor *and* Collage City
as prescription: these opposites,
involving the guarantees of both law
and freedom, should surely constitute
the dialectic of the future, rather
than any total surrender either to
scientific 'certainties' or the simple
vagaries of the *ad hoc*. The
disintegration of modern architecture
seems to call for such a strategy; an
enlightened pluralism seems to
invite; and, possibly, even common
sense concurs.

Notes

INTRODUCTION

1 Aristotle, *Nicomachean Ethics*, Book I para iii.

UTOPIA: DECLINE AND FALL?

1 We are indebted to Ian Boyd Whyte for calling to our attention this statement of Finsterlin's of 1919 which was republished in the catalogue of the Gläserne Kette exhibition (organized by O. M. Ungers, Berlin, 1963).

2 Frank Lloyd Wright, *A Testament*, New York, 1954, p.24.

3 Le Corbusier, *The Radiant City*, New York, 1964, p.143.

4 Karl Mannheim, *Ideology and Utopia*, New York, n.d., p.213. First published in 1936 in the International Library of Psychology, Philosophy and Scientific Method.

5 Judith Shklaar, 'The Political Theory of Utopia: From Melancholy to Nostalgia', *Daedalus*, Spring 1965, p.369.

6 For the André image we are indebted to Françoise Choay, *The Modern City: Planning in the Nineteenth Century*, New York 1969; but, unhappily and so far as we can discover, André remains a mere name—without dates or any further information. He is not listed in the *Dictionnaire de Biographie Française*; and, according to Mme. Choay, since her publication of this utopia, even the engraving itself has vanished from the Bibliothèque Nationale.

7 Henri de Saint-Simon, *Lettres d'un habitant de Genève à ses contemporains*, Geneva, 1803, republished in *Oeuvres de Saint-Simon et d'Enfantin*, Paris, 1865-78, Vol.XV.

8 The motto of Saint-Simon, *Opinions littéraires et philosophiques*, Paris, 1825. Also the motto of the Saint-Simonian periodical, *Le Producteur*, 1825-6.

9 Gabriel-Désiré Laverdant, *De La Mission de l'Art et du Rôle des Artistes*, Paris, 1845, quoted from Renato Poggioli, *The Theory of the Avant-Garde*, Cambridge, Mass., and London, 1968.

10 Léon Halévy, *Le Producteur*, Vol.I, p.399; Vol.III, pp.110 and 526.

11 Edmund Burke, *Reflections on the Revolution in France*, 1790, World Classics Ed., 1950.

12 William Morris, *News from Nowhere*, New York, 1890, London, 1891.

13 Burke, op.cit., p.186.

14 We allude to Burke's *Philosophical Inquiry into Our Ideas of the Sublime and the Beautiful*, London, 1756.

15 Burke, ibid, p.109.

16 Burke, ibid, pp.105-6.

17 *Oeuvres de Saint-Simon et d'Enfantin*, Vol.XX, pp.199-200.

18 It would be absurd on our part to pretend that what follows is any very specific scrutiny of Hegel. We have attempted to be conscientious; but are also obliged to concede fatigue. Our primary interest is, obviously, far from philosophical, but what we here attempt is a stipulation of Hegel's enormous, and generally unacknowledged importance to modern architecture.

19 Ludwig Mies Van der Rohe, G. No. 1 (bibliog. 2) 1923, quoted from Philip Johnson, *Mies Van der Rohe*, New York, 1947; Walter Gropius, *Scope of Total Architecture*, New York, 1955, p.61; Le Corbusier, *The Radiant City*, New York, 1964, p.28, from the CIAM Manifesto of 1928.

20 F. W. Nietzsche, *The Twilight of the Idols*, Chapter entitled 'Skirmishes in a War with the Age' section 38.

21 F. T. Marinetti, from the *Futurist Manifesto*, 1909, Proposition 9.

22 Walter Gropius, *The New Architecture and the Bauhaus*, London, 1935, p.48.

23 Le Corbusier, *Towards a New Architecture*, London, 1927, pp.14, 251.

AFTER THE MILLENNIUM

1 This reference to Kenneth Burke is approximate and its source appears now entirely to resist accurate recall.

2 The devotees of Futurism have, on the whole, been characteristically unwilling to advertise (or even scrutinize) the Marinetti-Mussolini relationship; but, at the risk of exaggerating its importance, one may still think of Marinetti's great—even superb—eulogium of the Duce:

built *all'italiana*, designed by inspired and brutal hands, forged, carved to the model of the mighty rocks of our peninsula.
Square crushing jaws. Scornful jutting lips that spit with defiance and swagger on everything slow, pedantic and finicking. Massive rock-like head, but the ultradynamic eyes dart with the speed of automobiles racing on the Lombard plains. To right and left flashes the gleaming cornea of a wolf.

and later:
... rising to speak, he bends forward his masterful head, like a squared off projectile, package full of gunpowder, the cubic will of the State.
But he lowers it in conclusion, ready to smash the question head on or, better, to gore it like a bull. Futurist eloquence well masticated by teeth of steel...

and still later:
His will splits the crowd like a swift antisubmarine beat, an exploding torpedo. Rash but sure, because his elastic good sense has accurately judged the distance. Without cruelty, because his vibrant fresh lyric childlike sensibility laughs. I remember how he smiled, like a happy infant, as he counted off twenty shots from his enormous revolver into the policeman's kiosk on the Via Paolo di Cannobio.

From *Marinetti and Futurism*, 1929, quoted from R. W. Flint, *Marinetti, Selected Writings*, New York, 1971.

3 Francoise Choay, *The Modern City: Planning in the Nineteenth Century*, New York, 1969.

4 Jacob B. Bakema, lecture at Cornell University, Spring 1972.

5 Giancarlo de Carlo, seminar at Cornell University, Spring 1972.

6 See, for instance, the criticism of Alan Colquhoun, 'Centraal Beheer, Apeldoorn, Holland', *Architecture Plus*, Sept.-Oct. 1974.

7 Robert Venturi reported in Paul Goldberger, 'Mickey Mouse Teaches the Architects', *New York Times Magazine*, 22 October, 1972.

8 ed. Emilio Ambasz, *Italy: The New Domestic Landscape*, New York, 1972, p.249.

9 Ambasz, ibid., p.247.

10 Ambasz, ibid., p.248.

11 From a Disney World brochure.

12 Paul Goldberger, op.cit.

13 We think of many locations but, particularly, of Owego, New York and Lockhart, Texas.

14 Ambasz, op. cit., p.250.

15 Of interest in this context could be Edmund Burke's 'Liberty, too, must be limited in order to be possessed', from *A Letter From Burke to the Sheriffs of Bristol on the Affairs of America*, London, 1777, *The Works of the Right Honourable Edmund Burke*, London, 1845, p.217.

16 Frances Yates, *The Art of Memory*, London and Chicago, 1966.

CRISIS OF THE OBJECT: PREDICAMENT OF TEXTURE

1 Le Corbusier, *The Home of Man*, London, 1948, pp.91, 96.

2 Lewis Mumford, *The Culture of Cities*, London, 1940, p.136.

3 Siegfried Giedion, *Space, Time and Architecture*, Cambridge, Mass., 1941, p.524.

4 Le Corbusier, *Towards a New Architecture*, London, 1927, p.167.

5 Point XIV of Van Doesburg's Madrid lecture of 1930; but this statement was incipient in 1924: 'In contrast to frontality sanctified by a rigid static concept of life, the new architecture offers a plastic wealth of multifaceted temporal and spatial effects.' *De Stijl*, Vol. VI, No.6-7, p.80.

6 Le Corbusier, *La Charte d'Athènes*, Paris, 1943. English translation, Anthony Eardley, *The Athens Charter*, New York, 1973.

7 J. Tyrwhitt, J. L. Sert and E. N. Rogers (eds.), *The Heart of the City: Towards the Humanisation of Urban Life*, New York, 1951, London, 1952.

8 Benjamin Disraeli, *Tancred*, London, 1847.

9 Alexander Tzonis, *Towards a Non-Oppressive Environment*, Boston, 1972.

10 Oscar Newman, *Defensible Space*, New York and London, 1972, *Architectural Design for Crime Prevention*, Washington, 1973. Newman offers pragmatic justification for what, in any case, ought to be normative procedure; but his inference (surely correct) that spatial dispositions may operate to prevent crime is an argument distressingly far removed from the more classical supposition that the

purposes of architecture are intimately related with the idea of the good society.

11 Robert Venturi, *Complexity and Contradiction in Architecture*, The Museum of Modern Art Papers on Architecture I, New York, 1966.

12 Le Corbusier, *Oeuvre Complète 1938-46*, Zurich, 1946, p.171. The statement: 'it is a language of proportions which makes evil difficult and good easy' is, supposedly, Albert Einstein's reaction to the Modulor.

COLLISION CITY AND THE POLITICS OF BRICOLAGE

1 Walter Gropius, *Scope of Total Architecture*, New York, 1955, p.91.

2 Thomas More, *Utopia*, 1516.

3 Isaiah Berlin, *The Hedgehog and the Fox*, London, 1953; New York, 1957, p.7.

4 Berlin, ibid., p.10.

5 Berlin, ibid., p.11.

6 William Jordy, 'The Symbolic Essence of Modern European Architecture of the Twenties and its Continuing Influence, *Journal of the Society of Architectural Historians*, Vol.XXII, No.3, 1963.

7 Karl Popper, *Logik der Forschung*, Vienna, 1934. English translation, *The Logic of Scientific Discovery*, London, 1959; *The Open Society and its Enemies*, London, 1945; *The Poverty of Historicism*, London, 1957.

8 Christopher Alexander, *Notes on the Synthesis of Form*, Cambridge, Mass., 1964. The attempted revival of Positivism in the 1960s—at a time when it might have been supposed to be extinct and its arguments long ago demolished—will surely, in the course of time, begin to present itself as one of the more interesting architectural curiosities of the twentieth century.

9 Claude Lévi-Strauss, *The Savage Mind*, London, 1966; New York, 1969, p.16.

10 Lévi-Strauss, ibid, p.16.

11 Le Corbusier, *Towards a New Architecture*, London, 1927, pp.18-19.

12 Lévi-Strauss, op. cit., p.17.

13 Lévi-Strauss, ibid., p.22.

14 Lévi-Strauss, ibid., p.19.

15 Lévi-Strauss, ibid., p.22.

16 The possibilities of an exponential, progressive dialectic—whether Marxian or Hegelian—are not here assumed to be 'useful'.

17 Frederick Law Olmsted and James R. Croes, *Preliminary Report of the Landscape Architect and the Civil and Topographical Engineer, Upon the Laying Out of the Twenty-third and Twenty-fourth Wards*, City of New York, Doc. No. 72, Board of Public Parks, 1877. Extracted from S. B. Sutton (ed.), *Civilizing American Cities*, Cambridge, Mass., 1971.

18 We are indebted for this image to Charles Jencks, *Modern Movements in Architecture*, New York and London, 1973.

19 Alexis de Tocqueville, *Democracy in America*, translation, Henry Reeve, London, 1835-40; New York, 1848, part 2, p.347.

COLLAGE CITY AND THE RECONQUEST OF TIME

1 Ernest Cassirer, *Philosophy of Symbolic Forms*, trans Ralph Manheim, New Haven and London 1953, and, for instance, Suzanne Langer, *Philosophy in a New Key*, Cambridge, Mass., 1942. But also—and not so incidentally—the whole Warburgian tradition should surely here be cited.

2 Particularly, Karl Popper, 'Utopia and Violence', 1947; and 'Towards a Rational Theory of Tradition', 1948. Published in *Conjectures and Refutations*, London and New York, 1962.

3 Popper, ibid., pp.120-35.

4 Popper, ibid., pp.355-63.

5 *Public Papers of the Presidents of the United States, Richard Nixon, 1969*. No. 265. Statement of the Establishment of the National Goals Research Staff.

6 Edward Surtz, S.J., *St. Thomas More: Utopia*, New Haven and London, 1964, pp.vii-viii.

7 At least such an idea, or so we believe, is reported in one of the earlier volumes of *La Revue Generale de L'Architecture*—though at the time of writing this note, the exact location of the source seems to evade our retrieval. In any case, a reading of such a document as Emmanuel de Las Cases, *Mémorial de Sainte Hélène* will provide at least some intimations of such a meditated policy. Napoleon's conversations at Longwood were mostly of a military or political concern; but, from time to time, matters of architecture and urbanism did arise and, then,

the drift of thought is characteristic. Napoleon is concerned with 'practical' performance (harbours, canals, water supply); but he is concerned, quite as much, with 'representational' gesture. And thus from Las Cases, ed. Paris 1956, the following quotations may be suggestive:

On Paris, Vol I, p.403.

Si le ciel, alors, continuait-il, m'eût accordé quelques années, assurément j'aurais fait de Paris la capitale de l'univers et de toute la France un véritable roman.

On Rome, Vol I p.431.

L'Empereur disait qui si Rome fût restée sous sa domination, elle fût sortie de ses ruines; il se proposait de la nettoyer de tous ses décombres, de restaurer tout ce qui eût été possible, etc. Il ne doutait pas que le même esprit s' étendant dans le voisinage, il eût pu en être en quelque sorte de même d 'Herculaneum et de Pompeia.

On Versailles, Vol I, p.970.

De ces beaux bosquets, je chassais toutes ces nymphes de mauvais goût…et je les remplaçais par des panoramas, en maçonnerie, de toutes les capitales où nous étions entrés victorieux, de toutes les célèbres batailles qui avaient illustré nos armes. C' eût été autant de monuments éternels de nos triomphes et de notre gloire nationale, posés à la porte de la capitale de l'Europe, laquelle ne pouvait manquer d 'être visitée par force du reste de l'univers.

And, finally, Vol II, p.154,

Il regrettait fort, du reste, de n' avoir pas fait construire un temple égyptien à Paris: c 'était un monument, disait-il, dont il voudrait avoir enrichi la capitale, etc.

But the notion of the city as museum, as a monument to the state and a representative of its culture, as an index and an instrument of education, which might seem to be implicit in Neo-Classical idealism also receives a microcosmic reflection in the notion of the house as museum; and we think here of Thomas Hope, Sir John Soane, Karl Friedrich Schinkel and, possibly, John Nash. For the Egyptian temple which Napoleon wished to have built in Paris, and which would have 'enriched' the capital, substitute the sarcophagus of Seti I with which Soane succeeded in 'enriching' his own domestic basement and the analogy begins to take shape. Add Soane's Parlour of Padre Giovanni and his Shakespeare Recess to Hope's Indian Room and Flaxman Cabinet (see David Watkin, *Thomas Hope and the Neo-Classical Idea*, London 1968) and the traces of what Schinkel was to attempt in Berlin and Potsdam are abundantly present. Indeed we are surprised that the category: city as museum, with its sub-category the 'museum street' (visible in places so far apart as Athens and Washington) has, so far, remained unidentified.

8 Claude Lévi-Strauss, *The Savage Mind*, London, 1966; New York, 1969, p.30. Also refer to Claude Lévi-Strauss, *The Raw and the Cooked*, New York, 1969, London 1970.

9 Alfred Barr, *Picasso: Fifty Years of his Art*, New York, 1946, pp.270-1.

10 Alfred Barr, ibid., p.241.

11 Lévi-Strauss, op. cit., p.11.

12 Barr, op. cit., p.79.

13 Barr, ibid, p.79.

14 Abraham Cowley, *Lives of English Poets, Works of Samuel Johnson* Ll.D., London, 1823, Vol 9, p.20.

15 At this stage, one thinks of the observations of Mr. Justice Brandeis: 'The irresistible is often only that which is not resisted'.

16 F. T. Marinetti, from the *Futurist Manifesto*, 1909 and from appendix to A. Beltramelli, *L'Uomo nuvo*, Milan, 1923. Both quotations extracted from James Joll, *Intellectuals in Politics*, London and New York, 1960.

17 Barr, op. cit., p.271.

18 St. Paul, *Epistle to the Romans*, 5:20.

19 Renato Poggioli, *The Theory of the Avant-Garde*, Cambridge, Mass., and London, 1968, p.219.

20 We are indebted to Kenneth Frampton for this quotation from Hannah Ahrendt. He is unable to specify its source.

21 O. M. Ungers, a much repeated remark addressed to students at Cornell University, c. 1969-70.

22 Samuel Johnson, *The Rambler*, no.194 (Saturday, 25 January 1752).

Index to text

Index to Illustrations

Sources and Credits

Reference is by page number.
i, 119 right Tom Schumacher;
26 The Royal Institute of British
Architects, London; iii, 3, 5 above,
17, 30, 51 right, 59, 67 below,
69 top right, 70 above and below
right, 71, 72 above, 73 below,
78 bottom, 92, 138, 139, 140,
141, © SPADEM; iv, 87, 108-111
Museo della Civiltà Romana and
Fototeca Unione; 7 below
Time-Life; 16 Yale University
Library; 23 below, 24, 25 Clichés
des Musées Nationaux, Paris;
34-35 from The Concise
Townscape, The Architectural
Press, London, 1971; 39
Cumbernauld Development
Corporation; 41 right, 98 from
A Decade of Architecture and Urban
Design, Karl Kramer Verlag,
Stuttgart; 42 below © William A.
Garnett, from N. A. Owings, The
American Aesthetic, 1969, by
permission of Harper & Row,
Publishers. Inc., New York;
© 53 Ewart Johns, from British
Townscape, Edward Arnold,
London, 1965; 54, 133 top from
S. Giedion, Space, Time and
Architecture, 1941; 55 below
KLM Aerocarto; 57 left from
Walter Gropius, Scope of Total
Architecture, Allen & Unwin,
London, 1956; 57 above right
Collection Bequest Nelly Van
Doesburg; 58, 70 below left
Artemis Verlag, Zurich; 62, 63, 81
right, 83, 131, 168 above, 170
above Wayne Copper; 69 below
right Mansell Collection; 70 below
right, 71 Studio Chevojon; 74-75
Stuart Cohen and Steven Hurtt;
76 below left Alinari; 76 below
right Anderson; 78 third below top,
141 top right Lucien Hervé; 80
above right M. Dennis; 81 left above
cliché Levy-Neurdein; 88 cliché
R. Henrard, from E. de Ganay,
André le Nostre, Editions Vincent
Fréal, Paris, 1962; 96 below from
Notes on Synthesis of Form,
Harvard U.P., Cambridge, Mass.;
102, 103 Susie Kim; 115
Collection Mr. and Mrs. Burton
Tremaine; 119 left, 146-147
Philip Rawson, Tantra, the Indian
Cult of Ecstasy, Thames & Hudson,
London, 1973; 126, 129 top left
Münchner Stadtmuseum; 127, 130
Bayerisches Nationalmuseum;
126, 127, 128, 129 top left,
second left from top, third left from
top, top right, 134 left from
Oswald Hederer, Leo von Klenze,
George D. W. Callwey, Munich,
1964; 129 below, 133 bottom,
135 below right from S. Giedion,
Spatbarocker und Romantischer
Klassizismus, Munich, 1922;
133 centre by courtesy of the St.
Pancras Public Library; 135
below left from Bruno Carl,
Klassiziissmus, Verlag Berichthaus,
Zurich, 1963; 142 Architectural
Review and Dell & Wainwright;
150 Servizio fotographico del
Commune di Roma; 152 above
T. Reynolds Williams; 152 below
COI Crown Copyright; 155 from
Vitale E. Ghianda, Genova Strada
Nuova, Genoa, 1967; 160 Museo
della Civiltà Romana; 161 above
The American School of Classical
Studies at Athens; 161 below from
Roberto Pane, Palladio, Electra
Editrice, Milan, 1952; 163 below
Italo Ballarin, from Piazza San
Marco, Marsilio Editori, Venice,
1970; 165 Touring Club
Italiano, 1972; 168 below, 169,
171 below from M. Dennis and
K. Herdeg, Urban Precedents,
Ithaca, 1974; 170 below from
N. Ardalan and L. Bakhtair, The
Sense of Unity, University of
Chicago Press, 1973; 171 above
from K. Herdeg, Formal Structure
in Indian Architecture, Ithaca,
1967; 172 top from Architectural
Plus, New York, September 1967;
172 left from R. Venturi, Denise
Scott Brown, and Steven Izenour,
Learning from Las Vegas, MIT
Press, 1972; 172 below right
Elliott Erwitt, from Ivan
Chermayeff, Observations on
American Architecture, Viking
Press, New York, 1972; 173 top
and bottom left NASA; 173 centre
and bottom right from M. Parent
and J. Verroust, Vauban, Editions
Jacques Fréal, Paris, 1971; 179
above Parma Galleria Nazionale;
below from Goodwood House—by
courtesy of the Trustees; 178 Tate
Gallery, London; 180 Collection
the Earl of Derby; 181 Musée du
Louvre, cliché des Musées
Nationaux, Paris.

Acknowledgements

Except for minor emendations,
mostly prompted by Judith
Holliday and Joel Bostick, the text
of this essay was completed in
December 1973; but the collection
of illustrations was quite another
campaign and, in this area, we
have to thank Jose Gelabert, Susan
Lermon and, particularly, Richard
Becherer. Some two thirds of the
illustrations were made by those
exceptional photographers Hadley
and Gertrude Smith of Ithaca,
New York who were, as always,
rocks of reliability and we are
immensely grateful for their work.
Roger Davies was a responsive
and sensitive designer and stepped
resourcefully into the role of
producer at a time when the
book's progress towards
publication seemed in doubt. To
Dorothy Rowe our obligation is
not to be estimated. Indeed it
would be probably true to say
that, without her trans-Atlantic
insistence and supervision, the
appearance of this book would
have been even more belated.

First MIT Press paperback edition, 1983

Copyright © 1978 by
The Massachusetts Institute of
Technology

Library of Congress Cataloging
in Publication Data
Rowe, Colin.
Collage city.
Includes bibliographical references
and indexes.
1. City planning. 2. Functionalism
(Architecture). 3. Eclecticism in
architecture. 4. Architecture,
Modern—20th century.
I. Koetter, Fred, joint author.
II. Title.
NA9050.R68 711'.4 78-60990
ISBN-13: 978-0-262-18086-3
(hc. : alk. paper) — 978-0-262-
68042-4 (pbk. : alk. paper)
ISBN-10: 0-262-18086-3 (hc.
: alk. paper) — 0-262-68042-4
(pbk. : alk. paper)

20 19 18 17 16 15